THE WHOLE TRUTH

How Banks Weaponised Lending, Accountants Monetised Ignorance and we ended up in a Sub 1% Economy

Peter Crowley

CONTENTS

INTRODUCTION 1

1. HOW THE SMES SAW IT 15

2. HOW THE BANKS SAW IT 27

3. HOW THE MARKET SAW IT 47

4. HOW THE BANKS THEN SAW IT 57

5. HOW THE SMES THEN SAW IT 69

6. HOW THE FSA SAW IT 79

7. HOW THE MPS SAW IT 93

8. HOW THE EX SALESMEN SEE IT 105

9. HOW THE FCA/PRA (AND OTHER REGULATORS) SAW IT 115

10. HOW THE LAWYERS SEE IT 133

11. HOW THE ACCOUNTANTS SAW IT 143

12. HOW THE SENIOR COURTS MAY SEE IT 155

APPENDIX A: DARA O'BRIAIN'S CHIP GAME - 'SCHOOL OF HARD SUMS' 167

APPENDIX B: TYPICAL PRESENTATION SLIDES 169

INTRODUCTION

"Stop, stop, stop!' he cried; "stop talking a minute, for I see half. Will God give me strength? Will my brain make the one jump and see all? Heaven help me! I used to be fairly good at thinking. . . Will my head split - or will it see? I see half - I only see half."

G.K. Chesterton — The Innocence of Father Brown

1

"The interest rate swap scandal has cost small businesses dear. Many had no concept of the instrument they were being pressured to buy. This applies to embedded swaps as much as standalone products. The response by the FSA and FCA has been inadequate. If, as they claim, the regulators do not have the power to deal with these abuses, then it is for the Government and Parliament to ensure that the regulators have the powers they need to enable restitution to be made for this egregious mis-selling."

-Parliamentary Commission on Banking Standards – June 2013

"The UK government has accepted arguments, championed by the Law Society, that UK retail banks should be able to offer derivatives to business customers.

The Law Society has consistently argued to the Independent Commission on Banking and HM Treasury that retail banks should be able to offer derivative products to their business customers.

Derivatives can play a vital role in supporting everyday business activity, helping reduce business uncertainty such as fluctuations in exchange and interest rates and volatile commodity prices when used to hedge risk. Law Society Chief Executive Desmond Hudson said it was a real win for businesses and the wider UK economy which would have been disadvantaged by a less competitive banking environment.

'The Law Society played a crucial role by harnessing expertise from our members who specialise in banking law and providing compelling evidence and robust analysis of the impact of the government's proposals.'"

- Law Society Press Release – May 2013

"I cannot accept that there does not exist an expertise in the practice of banks in selling IRHPs to retail customers. A distinction does need to be drawn between evidence of accepted practice which is admissible, and evidence which amounts to no more than the expert's opinion of what he or she would have done in the circumstances, which is not admissible. But the sale of derivatives by banks to individual customers as a hedge for loan transactions, although a comparatively new phenomenon, has been recognised as highly regulated activity over the past 10-15 years. It is a specialist niche in lending by the major banks, for which their employees have, or ought to have been, specially trained. I am presently satisfied that there is, or is likely to be a body of practice that has grown up in the banking industry as to how these derivatives should be sold, and that there is a broad division in such practice between sales to retail customers and sales to professional customers and market counter-parties. To that extent, I am fortified in this conclusion by the fact that the parties in the swap cases, where I have already directed that there should be expert evidence, appear to have had no difficulty in identifying individuals able to give the relevant expert evidence."

Quoted by Mrs Justice Rose DBE - [2014] EWHC 2818
– attributed to Judge Havelock-Allan QC.

* * *

Interest rate swap mis-selling was a lot worse than either pension or PPI mis-selling, because the products were *actually designed to do damage.* With the other two scams, it could be argued that they were selling the right products to the wrong people. However, derivatives, or swaps were *deployed* by banks to expose clients to *what they (banks) knew to be increased risk.*

Immediately after a swap was purchased, it reduced the creditworthiness of the client. Weirdly enough, even a cap could do the same if it was substantially overpriced, as the reduction in the buyer's capital outweighs the benefit of protection against a rise in interest rates, which the market then valued at a relative pittance. But, at least then the immediate damage is more transparent, and easier to identify.

Most of those involved in swaps mis-selling did not understand what was going on. Of the ones who understood what was going on, few, if any, have described in detail what was actually wrong with the practice. Hence my title, "The Whole Truth", as I both understand and tell all that I know.

The whole subject is smothered in confusion, and many pundits make comments which are at worst misleading and at best part truth concealing, sometimes inadvertently, the key truths.

One fact that became clear at an early stage was that some of the 'big four' banks were laughing at the clients, whom they believed that they had swindled. There followed much debate, as clearly there was a disconnect between this behaviour and the methods they had used to sell the products:

- the slides which excluded or played down the serious downsides of the products that the banks pushed.
- the commission driven salesforces.
- the highly technical nature of the products, (where the *operation* might be simple, but the *valuation and risk issues* were substantially obscure, even to many senior bank executives).

A process that a superficial assessment would indicate was a licence to print money; turned out to create nightmares for not only the hapless purchasers, but also the banks who sold them; and then the UK economy as a whole. In effect, while those banks were deceiving their clients, they were deceiving themselves by ignoring risks that had been defined formally by EU banking regulators; and which those self-same banks actually described as risks in *their own* Reports and Accounts. Clearly, this indicates a serious breakdown between the technical and supervisory sides of banking. Individuals who are 'clever' enough to generate products from opaque sources are encouraged to do so, with little dispassionate consideration of the sources of those profits. External regulators also appeared to have given the nod to these products and their selling processes, basing their acceptability tests solely on a bank's day 1 profits. The result is a build-up of risk within both companies and banks, which accumulates into the national financial system. The worst aspect is that this risk has been artificially created, and exploits the difference between the perception of the view of fixed interest rates within the banking industry (or "those in the know"); and those in the external financial community, primarily via the accountancy profession (or "the outsiders").

One of the most misleading factors has been the definition of 'sophistication' of a customer; an artificial concept based on the size of a business, rather than the awareness of its executives, or the availability of informed, unbiased advice; and susceptibility to misinformation. This issue has seriously clouded the dissemination of understanding of what actually happened during the mis-selling period (primarily 2006 to 2009) and resulted in a much criticised and 'unsophisticated' regulatory review process, which banks have easily been able to distort to their own advantage. This has exacerbated the dissatisfaction of the victims, which has escalated to result in an All Party Parliamentary Group investigation on the issue of swaps mis-selling, and, after a number of years, commanded sustained attention from the Treasury Select Committee. It also generated well supported early day motions in the House of Commons. One spokesman for a group of victims (whose companies are now insolvent) attended a meeting at 10 Downing Street recently - and so the controversy clearly continues.

What ended up as a very successful con, was almost certainly developed in brainstorming sessions within the major banks, incorporating US banking techniques, and were probably converted to workable practices in the UK with the assistance of major "accountant/ management consultants". (I call these "AMC"s.) This reflects the definition of sophistication that I would prefer to use, which incorporates awareness, experience, and the ability to conceptualise. A full understanding is difficult without sustained discussion or reflection, and hence to understand what was actually wrong with what was done requires adequate time, energy, and mental application.

For what has been a very clever scam, the attention paid to it by regulators and public commentators, has been slight. Many superficial assessments have been made, which gloss over the most important facts. As far as the main media, national broadcasters and the national press (although nowadays supplemented by social media) are concerned, broad summaries are necessary to cater for their readers and viewers who have limited time and attention span. The expression "it was not explained to customers that they would have to pay out if interest rates fell" is repeated time and time again. This is actually wrong, as presentations generally brought out the payment issues clearly. What was concealed, and most probably deliberately, is that there were risks in excess of those of future payment rules, *even if the customers made all of the payments on time.*

Much of the criticism has been directed towards derivative contracts in general. Overall, derivatives can be used for several purposes, and meet a number of financial needs. They can be a useful product. For example, life assurance companies need to invest with regard to long term liabilities, and derivatives can be of assistance here. One knowledgeable commentator has written an article to suggest that if Equitable Life had used derivatives intelligently, it would have survived, and compares its fate with that of other life assurance companies that did use these contracts. Similarly, pension funds have long term liabilities, for which derivatives may be useful in matching – a number of funds do this, and the Pension Protection Fund also buys derivatives in volume. However, as far as a smaller investor or an SME is concerned, one of their strengths is also a weakness- the extreme flexibility in initial product design allows products to be designed not only to the detriment of the buyer, but where the initial cash flow can be pitched in his favour, hence hiding their true nature – then, once the deal has been agreed, the total lack of flexibility, apart from any options, which are usually set in favour of the bank. When the products presented and context in which they were sold to the bulk of purchasers are examined, the serious flaws in the sales and explanation processes are apparent.

To show how such a scam can be developed, I provide an example used to promote Dara O'Briain's 'School of Hard Sums':

"You and your mate have a bag containing 65 chips. You take turns to each take between one and seven chips, and the person who takes the last chip has to do a dance. Should you go first or second, and what dance would you do?"

The answer is shown in Appendix A, but, more importantly, I show you how you might profit from *hiding* your full knowledge.

The iniquities in the process were well known by 'those in the know' in the banks. I was chatting idly with a stranger with whom I was sharing a crowded pub a couple of weeks ago, who turned out to work in IT in a major European bank. When I mentioned the mis-selling process, he simply smirked, and said "Oh yeah – Protection". This sarcasm was more telling than any formal exposition I have ever heard or read.

The subtitle of this book includes "Monetising Ignorance". It was not just banks that profited from ignorance. Accountants, lawyers, surveyors and other "professions" were, and are, in on the game. I break ignorance down into two types – feigned and genuine. Clearly, some people knew something fishy was going on – but chose not to speak out. Also, what may have started off as genuine ignorance must have become feigned ignorance, as, for example, swap salesmen, realised that it was not a good idea to ask the boss certain questions.

So what was the process? In a nutshell, banks took what they defined as 'risk', packaged it up, and sold it to clients as 'hedging'. They knew that the risks would be particularly acute to the buyers, as the products were sold to firms and individuals taking out term loans, and were then not only exposed to the risks the loans generated (of which they were aware), but the loan covenants as part of the loan contracts were covertly also used as security ("collateralisation") for the derivatives sold.

The products were promoted as 'protection' against interest rate rises. However, when pricing up the products that were actually sold, the value of the premium needed to insure that risk in the market was modest. The plan, as was demonstrated by promotional material and sales we have investigated, was to get the purchaser to take on *downside* risk. The profit could then be the difference between two large amounts – positive and negative – which should ring massive warning bells. It is like a mix of healthy and unhealthy elements – compare selling a medicine consisting of vitamins and poison – and deliberately not explaining some of the risks contained in the poison.

The market in which these derivative products were traded was focussed on *market* risk i.e., capital gains and losses and not credit risk, or the soundness of market players' own ability to meet their financial promises. That is, it was possible to buy caps, floors, swaps and collars, but market participants would need to offer very solid guarantees that they could meet their commitments. Major banks could deal in these markets – small companies trying to operate directly would not be not welcome (having a high credit risk, compared with banks, or similar organisations).

As stated above, the whole precept of selling these products was based on a bank presenting products as protecting against the risk of rate rises, but the real motive for the sale was to turn the borrowers into underwriters for downside risk. As the derivatives markets showed a pessimistic outlook, with dealers offering lower and lower interest rates the further one goes into the future, it was clear that the market would pay well for those risks to be insured against. So the banks were therefore committing their clients to risk, then selling off this risk, taking a 'turn', and effectively matching borrowers against major market liabilities. One such end user was the Pension Protection Fund, who were exposed to the risks of interest rate falls.

As security for these derivatives, the banks relied on the covenants within the loans – that is why the derivative could not be allowed to remain on the client's books (i.e. allowed to continue) if the loan was repaid – the enforceability of loan covenants was needed to enforce the derivative's security requirements.

To cover the bank against any legal action should the downside risk crystallise, and the borrower not be satisfied with the bank's defence of what had been a misleading sales process, the bank introduced blanket disclaimers, primarily denying that they had been giving 'advice'. Advice has a particular connotation in the sale of financial products. But, reading the promotional literature, listening to recordings of sales pitches, and from voluminous anecdotal evidence from victims, it is clear that the products were promoted doggedly, and via protracted and sustained sales approaches.

Much store has been placed by banks, and reflected in the FCA review, as to whether 'the client first expressed a desire/interest in 'interest rate protection'. However, a moment's reflection reveals that to be nonsense. The banks' day to day managers (called Relationship Managers, or RMs) were primed and incentivised to raise 'interest rate risk' with clients. Clearly, for a variable rate borrower, the risk is that rates rise, not that they fall. Moreover, any client who is taking out or renewing a loan is unlikely to express indifference to any risk suggested by a bank if they are looking for loan finance, which is within the gift of the bank – they would then appear to be imprudent borrowers. From this, it is easy to fill in a fact find record form stating 'client showed an interest in interest rate protection'. This was part of the process of the bank protecting *itself* against possible future claims.

To the layman, fixed rate loans (at least, short term ones), may intuitively sound 'safer' than variable rate ones – it can be difficult to explain why banks see fixed rates as risk. From the earliest days, there has been a saying in banking, that a bank's risk was always the risk of lending long, and borrowing short. Borrowers from banks generally want to maximise the terms (subject to cost) of loans, as projects often take years to complete, while traditional bank depositors want access to their funds at short notice. Accordingly, banks can be exposed to rises in interest rates – say they lend long term, e.g. at 5% per annum, and borrow short term, at, say 4% per annum; the they earn a 1% per annum margin. If, subsequently, short term rates rise to 6%, they will need to raise the rates offered (or short term depositors will move their funds), and then the bank will make ongoing losses.

If, in contrast, the bank makes its loans on a variable rate basis, much of this problem disappears. The bank can link its ongoing interest charges to the market, and ensure it both maintains a reasonable margin, and stays competitive. Variable rates have become the lending standard since the rate volatility experienced in the early 1970s, apart from for short term loans.

Where many people find difficulty in understanding what happened is due to the 'Could they? ... Would they? ...' arguments, which represent two mental barriers. 'Could they' refers to the difficulty of understanding that it is possible to create products with the intention and capability of doing damage – i.e. designed to generate negative benefits - 'Would they' refers to whether a bank's staff would actually be so dishonest to promote and sell such products, with key facts concealed. Unfortunately, in both cases, the answer is 'yes'.

To illustrate what happened, each chapter is followed by an example of a mis-sale (or sale, depending on your point of view.) This includes some technical detail, which I have tried to simplify as much as possible. Some readers will find it confusing, but, if you do, you are not alone – the topic merits re-reading more than once in order to get a full understanding.

The first chapter describes the character and attitudes of the group of UK SMEs as a whole, with particular attention paid to their attitude towards responsible borrowing and investment in their businesses.

But first...

EXAMPLE
MR GREG VINYARD, BARCLAYS BANK

The first real life client we met was Mr Greg Vinyard. His company, Barrel Resolve, which provided secure storage, had been sold a 25-year swap at 4.78% by Barclays Bank in March 2006 in connection with a property loan. The notional (initial size) of the swap was £1 million, amortising. The bank made a gross profit of £33,000 on day one of the deal. This consisted of client benefit of value £1,400 on the day of sale, less bank benefit of £34,400, as at that date.

His story was that his regular RM (Relationship Manager – they used to be known as Branch Managers) took him and his wife to the bank's offices in Canary Wharf, where after they were shown a PowerPoint presentation, the product was sold to them. At the conclusion, the RM said "I didn't understand any of that - but what I do understand is that I'm now allowed to buy you a good lunch".

The £33,000 represented the bank's day 1 profits due to the net discounting of cash flows, and the bank presumably hoped that future interest rates would behave within certain limits (if they didn't, that was the customer's lookout). The bank had insured itself against the risk of rates rising, to the degree that the cap would have been breached, at a cost of £1,400; so all would have been well. But if rates fell, there would be a crystallisation of risks to the customers' business that *were in excess of the need to make a series of payments at future points in time.*

In March 2006, Base Rate was 4.5%. So, without any derivative, the repayments on a £1,000,000 loan would be about £5,620 per month (ignoring, for the moment, the interest rate loading). Plus, around £230 per month initially for the swap, equal a total of £5,850.

When interest rates fall, it is standard practice for a lender to reschedule the loan so the capital is all paid off on the same date as before. So, when interest rates fell to ½% in March 2009, the repayments did NOT fall to 1/9 of their former size (½% is one ninth of 4.5%). Rather, they would fall to about £3,550, or a much higher 63% of the former level.

HOWEVER, the swap payments go up by a factor of over 15! That is by the ratio of (4.78% - 0.5%) / (4.78% - 4.5%) = 4.28% / 0.28% = 15.29 times. The swap now costs him £3,560 per month.

So his total monthly outgoing is now: £3,550 + £3,560 = £7,120

This has gone up by £7,120 - £5,850, an increase of £1,270, or some 22%. Some hedging!

Second, interest rate movements aren't random, unlike other loan related risks that are usually insured, e.g. the occurrence of, say, company director mortality (loss of key man risk), and factory fires (operating risk); low interest rates usually coincide with a depressed economy, or with reduced sales levels nationally, *so the increased payments come at a time when they are hardest to meet.*

The swap is making the business *less creditworthy*, and so future refinancing will be *harder* to achieve.

Needless to say, the bank would have known beforehand that if interest rates fell this was likely to happen. FCA Principle 8 states:

"A firm must manage conflicts of interest fairly, both interest between itself and its customers and between a customer and another client".

However, banks clearly feel free to ignore this when dealing with businesses, and the FCA winked, and still winks, at this.

In fact, the business becomes less creditworthy from the moment the derivative is taken out. This is not only because the swap starts off as a financial drag on the business (£33,000 at "accountants' fair value"), but because of three other reasons:

a) its value may get worse, a lot worse, at short notice,
b) the bank needs 'collateral' to cover the risk of this (arrangements for collateralisation were not generally disclosed), and
c) the purchaser is completely unaware of these risks, and the bank makes no effort to enlighten him – all the bank generally tells him is that his business has become poorer for unexplained reasons, and he needs to pay higher loan interest, and other charges.

Attempts to refinance in a recession are always difficult, and because of the swap, his business would be at the back of the queue.

In this case, it ended reasonably happily, and Mr Vinyard got paid £220,000 under the FCA review in 2014, which looks like the amount of past payments under the swap. The swap was also cancelled. The review allocates 8% pa annum interest to allow for consequential loss, but does not explain or deal with all the factors above.

The sale was accompanied by a PowerPoint slide show – I have provided an anonymised version in Appendix B.

The graph overleaf shows something just as interesting – the actual effect of the swap on Mr Vinyard's business. I have looked at the position at the initial sale date, and for the eight-year period post sale. What is most interesting is not the on-going value of the derivative, but how the bank (and any other bank with which Mr Vinyard may try to refinance) would see this derivative mar his business.

GREG VINYARD - SWAP FROM BARCLAYS BANK

The following points are of interest:

1) The black line shows the "Fair Value" or market value of the derivative. The grey line includes also the collateralisation allowance. I have worked on the understanding that a standard approximation to this is 2% of the notional times the term. If this seems high, consider the figure quoted in the "Crestsign vs RBS" case:

"This, Mr Gillard explained, would earn the banks about £50,000 and would require a "credit line" or contingent liability of £640,000. A credit line is an internally used measure of a bank's exposure in a particular derivative transaction, and represents the maximum amount of credit the banks would be willing to extend to the borrower to cover the eventuality of default or payment of break costs."

A factor of about 13 times profit there, then. That swap was only a 10 year one, not like Mr Vinyard's 25-year product, which would be 2½ times worse.

2) At times, the derivative actually becomes an asset – but, unsurprisingly,

once the collateralisation is allowed for, the total remains negative, and will probably stay that way until the last months of the term.

3) The market value hits a historical low of around £100,000 when base rate dives to ½%. However, there was worse to come. By August 2012 we hit a low of £185,000. For the two years August 2011 to August 2013, the value is never better than £100,000.

4) The collateralisation contribution reduces as time expires – look at how the gap between grey and black lines decreases with time. However, this is not fast enough to ever reduce the gross capital requirement below £300,000 in this example. This shows the enormous hidden damage that the swap does to Barrell Resolve's balance sheet position.

5) The bank then has a dilemma. The economy has slowed, and property values have fallen. Almost certainly, the borrower cannot refinance with another lender – and his loan covenants are almost certainly broken. The bank planned to cover itself against this risk using the loan covenants to "cover" the swap. It cannot tell him the truth.

6) For a bank to have a significant volume of such clients on its books is an enormous capital drag. The solution to these banks was to find reasons to break up some clients, release the collateralisation reserve, and seize their assets to boost its depleted capital position. This explains the reported behaviour of the RBS "Global Recovery Group" ("GRG"); Lloyds TSB's "Business Support Unit" ("BSU"); and similar groups. Such behaviour reduces the strain on the bank's capital position.

Please note, I have used Bank of England data for the above calculations – banks will use specialist systems, which are more robust. However, my graphs show the key features.

1.
HOW THE SMES SAW IT

"But every clever crime is founded ultimately on some one quite simple fact—some fact that is not itself mysterious. The mystification comes in covering it up, in leading men's thoughts away from it."

G.K. Chesterton, The Innocence of Father Brown

SMEs, or 'Small to Medium Enterprises', comprise a business class which can be defined in more than one way. However, the image of a family company probably meets the picture that most of us have. In December 2014, Stephen Nickell of the Department of Budget Responsibility stated that –

> "SMEs are particularly vulnerable to changes to bank lending. Large companies, generally speaking, have access to alternatives to bank lending, the bond market and so on. Of course SMEs and small companies generally rely on *or have in the past* relied on the banking system." (My italics)

My definition of SME, then, is taken from how they run their finances, and sources of support for this. For the larger firm in this grouping, services from a treasury department, either in-house or on a consultancy basis should be available, and they would (or, at least, should) understand the key risks involved with derivatives. As we move down the scale towards the one-man band, supported by the high street accountancy firm, knowledge is likely to be far more limited, (even subsequent to recent changes in reporting requirements for derivatives). Most learning, and understanding, post the mis-selling period, is likely to come through experience. Unfortunately, for many, a single negative event can be fatal.

In general, SMEs are likely to be "unsophisticated", in terms of company borrowing, especially long term borrowing. By this, I do not mean the arbitrary classification based on size and profitability used by regulators – I will expand on this later. My own definition, I believe, is more consistent with what people would generally understand by that term.

When I met a number of the swap mis-selling SME claimants, certain qualities were apparent:

Business models were straightforward – services that they provided could usually be described in a single sentence.

Financially conservative – caution and attention to financial detail, combined with frequent and regular review of financial position, and tight control of expenditure.

Businesses had been developed over a sustained period – growth generated by focus on efficient customer service.

Accordingly, wealth had been built up – businesses operated with adequate resources to support operations, and were secure.

Significant property assets were common, with those properties often connected to the operation of the businesses themselves, or sometimes providing financial solidity with some of the aspects of a property holding company.

Businesses were run under the control of relatively few individuals-quite often a single individual – and were often family run businesses.

I have formed these impressions from discussions with many of these individuals, mostly within groups set up to address issues with derivative and fixed rate loan sales, social media contributions (such as Twitter), and blogs following articles in the national news.

HOW THEY WOULD EXPECT LENDING TO BE PROVIDED

Longer term SME clients of banks had formed relationships based on mutual trust. One powerful example is that of Mr Paul Adcock, whose firm, Adcock and Sons ("Adcocks") , had a relationship with Barclays Bank that went back around 100 years. Clearly, for such a relationship to last so long a high degree of honesty and integrity from both parties would have been required. The levels of service and the terms of loans would have needed to seem reasonable to Adcocks. Similarly, their repayment record, and prudent principles in running their business, would have encouraged Barclays to maintain and nurture that relationship. (Adcocks are covered in more detail in Chapter 6)

It is worth at this stage expounding on the principles on which both Adcocks and Barclays would have managed their mutual relationship:

1)   Loans should be made to be repaid.

It would have been a basic expectation of the relationship that the terms of loans provided to Adcocks would have been adhered to; especially in respect of repayment of interest and capital instalments when due. In a well-run business, those repayments would have been reserved for at an early stage, and therefore, business would not have had to strain itself to make the repayments.

Had Adcocks at any time 'got into difficulties' and struggled to make payments on time, Barclays would clearly have had the power to call in the loan; possibly bankrupting Adcocks in the process. But they would exercise discretion, based on a number of factors: prominently Adcocks' longer term prospects, the character of the borrower, and their past lending record.

2)   Interest charged depends on the creditworthiness of the borrower.

It has often been a bone of contention that smaller company borrowers get charged more in terms of interest rate than larger ones. This, unfortunately, relates to the fact that the risk of lending to a smaller company is higher, and the bank effectively takes an "insurance premium" from the interest rate charged, to cover itself against loss. If one pictures a bank lending to large groups of both small and large companies – if their experience of the smaller company group is that more of those loans get into difficulties, there needs to be some compensation to the bank for the higher risk. Along with this "risk premium", the bank also adds on a profit margin. It can be difficult for a borrower to separate what is the risk premium, and what is profit margin – but this is done by considering the overall rate of interest charged. The borrower can safely consider that each bank would rate his business in the same way; and that the total interest rate charged is a good assessment of whether any bank is overcharging. Also, an established relationship was in place, the borrower would be less inclined to re-broke his business, as long as the rate stayed reasonably competitive.

3)   Underwriting Gatekeeper.

Banks present themselves, and are regarded by borrowers, as gatekeepers. There is an expectation from any honest and open customer that the bank will not only examine the business prior to advancing the monies, but may also require on-going checks – mainly based on information generated from the annual report and accounts, but sometimes needed more frequently; which are mutually regarded as assurance that all is well with the loan. In addition, the borrower's business plans, and any profit and cash flow projections over the lifetime of the loan should be reviewed.
     This can be contrasted with the underwriting involved in a residential

mortgage, where the initial criteria are more stringent, but the subsequent behaviour of the borrower is largely ignored (as long as full repayments are made on time) – and self-reporting of any issue is relied upon. Post 2008, the initial criteria for residential mortgages have been beefed up, but no new on-going underwriting requirements have been imposed.

Clearly, if an SME finds his bank's initial or subsequent loan underwriting requirements too onerous, he has the right to refinance, and move his borrowing elsewhere.

The mutual hope is that the bank will stay competitive, and that, accordingly, the customer will then stay with the bank. However, there would also be a mutual expectation that transferability would be a possibility if a bank's charges got too far out of line with the market. As transferring a term loan would incur expenses, imposed by both the current and novating banks, the difference would need to be significant enough to justify the move.

There is a temptation for any lending bank to try and "lock in" any borrower, as it could then have a far greater leeway with charge and interest rate increases without the fear of competition. Interest rate swap sales achieved this aim. Clearly, borrowers would have avoided "swap selling banks" if the anticompetitive effect of those swaps had been explained to them.

Another tactic used by banks was to persuade clients (or insist) that all banking services, including management of all bank accounts, were run through that bank. While this can be a common tactic for all business service providers, it is particularly dangerous with banking, where a single bank can far more easily take a disproportionate control over the company. Any business nowadays would be most unwise to trust a single bank, and would be well advised to manage its business via more than one bank, once resources allow.

NEGOTIATION ATTITUDE

Traditionally, banks provided a level of client largesse when courting new business or maintaining their client relationships. Of course, this was always paid for via higher interest rates imposed, and other fees. There are no free lunches! While such methods are generally understood and broadly accepted by all parties, there came a realisation that clients were getting worse and worse deals, and that this apparent "largesse" generated a disproportionate future cost.

At two levels, a friend of mine, who runs a successful property operation, expressed it thus:

> "They gave us all skiing jackets - very nice design, but I reckon each one cost us about £1,000 in extra fees. Then they took some of us away for a skiing week end in the Alps – that cost me about £20,000...."

Of course, the packages accepted and fees paid are a matter for the parties involved, and the recipient of such largesse is unlikely to receive much sympathy in respect of his complaints. However, it is a tactic to be wary of.

At the top end of the scale is the case of London and West Country Estates vs. the Royal Bank of Scotland, which will hit the screens (sorry, courts) early in 2017. To quote the Western Morning News:

> "They (business owners Mike and Diane Hockin) were taken by RBS on a complimentary trip to Royal Ascot in June 2008 and shared a box with celebrities Katie Price and Peter Andre as the pink champagne flowed."

RBS sold a large derivative in conjunction with the loan they made to the company, which contributed to its bankruptcy.

While RBS is not accused of promoting the Bermudan swaps that they landed on the couple as a holiday, the barristers will be asking a lot of interesting questions at the hearings. The role of Ernst and Young as insolvency practitioners, and how they considered these swaps in their assessment of the company, is also of interest.

All of the above conceals the fact that a loan, in essence, is a commodity product - £1 of RBS's money lent is identical to £1 of Barclays or HSBC's cash (although, clearly, not from Ron and Reg - you need to be careful who you borrow from, for all the above reasons).

In the wake of the 2008 crash, and loss of belief in any degree of fair dealing from the major banks, a new type of lender, the "Peer to Peer lender" (or

"P2P lender"), has appeared in the marketplace. These firms rely on the internet to link up individual lenders and borrowers, and slice up their loans, so that a lender may provide funds to a large number of borrowers (the small amounts involved being beneath the levels that a bank would consider), and therefore help lenders to manage default risk (or "credit risk", as it is technically known); in a way that larger banks cannot. The benefits are passed onto both borrowers and lenders. Such organisations have received some public criticism, notably from Lord Adair Turner, who stated in the Financial Times in February 2016 that:

'P2P loans could be the source of losses that would "make the worst bankers look like absolute lending geniuses"'.

As Lord Turner was formerly the head of the FSA, the organisation charged with regulating banks' conduct, and solvency, and which failed so badly at that, it was ignominiously dissolved in April 2013, his views may need to be taken with a pinch of salt. However, every lending or borrowing process has its own risks, and these need to be understood before engaging with any of them.

SIMPLE PRODUCTS

What P2P lenders do provide is a simplified lending model, and this follows the lines promoted by Lord Thursoe, who was on the House of Commons Treasury Select Committee at the time. Lord Thursoe advocated a range of simple products, which could be understood by all, and could be safely promoted by the financial services industry. However, what seems simple is sometimes deceptively complex.

An example of this is the pension annuity product, which can now be investigated over the web. There are several websites, including one provided by the FCA, from which a potential annuity buyer can obtain the current rate for a variety of options. The area that is missing is that of medically underwritten annuities, whereby an improved rate might be available, based on the purchaser's particular medical condition. Clearly, for such purchasers, additional bespoke work needs to be done, as no two people, nor their medical conditions, are identical. However, for the healthy among us, the market can be assessed quickly and efficiently.

The upshot of a clearer understanding of the loan market, and greater awareness (and less automatic respect for banks), meant that more SMEs became capable and willing to negotiate between banks – this pushed margins down. This was also broadly in line with government expectations; where there was concern about the lack of competition in the banking services market.

Borrowers would then expect a level playing field – banks offering products based on the riskiness of that borrower (where you would expect similar views across banks) and based on that bank's own efficiency, and ability to source cheaper funds in the market for the benefit of its clients (expect a range of rates and charges, then) – would enhance the principle of market-based competition.

Clearly, some borrowers might conceal key facts about their business to either a) get a better interest rate or b) to get the loan in the first place – but I exclude these from consideration. I have covered this possibility in the "Lending and Borrowing Principles" section below.

BANKS' ADDITIONAL REQUIREMENTS AND SALES

Where any bank lends funds, prudence requires that it takes steps to protect its risk exposure, as far as that is practically possible.

A good example is a covenant requiring property insurance on a factory used as security for a loan. Should the factory burn down, or be otherwise damaged, the borrower's income is likely to be disrupted, and his ability to repay his loan reduced. The property insurance should (hopefully) provide immediate funds in order to return the business to a profitable state as soon as is possible and, accordingly, this insurance is a reasonable condition for a bank to impose.

Another likely requirement is Director's "Keyman" life insurance, where both lender and borrower are protected against the potential profit loss, due to the early and unexpected death of a member of the senior staff, which would then disrupt the business. The funds provided by the insurance in this event should cushion the effect of the loss, until new senior staff can be induced effectively into the roles.

In both cases above, products are available to cover the risks described, without exposing the insured to any additional risks. More specifically, there is a reasonable expectation that any of these products should enhance, and not degrade, the likelihood of the loan being repaid as per the original expectations described in the loan schedule.

It can be noted that derivative products were sold by banks as if they were similar to the above products – as "Hedging"," Insuring" or "Protecting" the loan. This, in substance, was clearly not the case with any of the derivative sales we have seen, as will be explained as we continue.

LENDING AND BORROWING PRINCIPLES

That "Loans should be made to be repaid" should go without saying. Accordingly, both income and capital covenants should be reasonable and mutually acceptable. The latter covenants are generally seen as conveying solidity, rather than something that is likely to be policed to the letter, especially during an economic downturn.

Accordingly, any SME would expect both parties to a loan agreement to put a high expectation on both:

a) Payments being made as they fall due, and
b) Its own security being adequate to see it through a reasonable range of financial difficulties, in all but extreme circumstances
c) Any of its own behaviour leading, or likely to lead, to a significant deterioration of covenant would not be acceptable, and
d) Clearly, nothing is perfect, so in extreme circumstances, "all bets may be off". In this case, one or both parties might resort to the courts.

I would point out that no-one has actually made these comments to me in so many words – I have inferred these principles from both general discussions, reviewing many loan covenant contracts, and common sense.

In summary, a SME would expect income and capital covenants to be part of the lending process, but income ones to be paramount – especially the continued practice of making payment when due (i.e., not being in default). This would correspond with most people's concept of "fair play", in bank lending.

The next chapter covers the motives and philosophies of the banks who sold interest rate swaps. Traditionally banks were trusted partners of SME's, willing to provide finance on commercial terms, but ensuring that loans were underwritten prudently, with adequate security in place. With increasing competitive pressure on margins, and the emergence of what initially seemed a fool proof money making scheme, banks started to hard sell (or legally insist) on "hedging" products, sold alongside the loan. Risks were deliberately concealed, and then a cover-all sales clause insisted that "The client is acting on his or her own responsibility, and is not advised by us".

EXAMPLE
CARL AND MARK CANTOR, THE FUN FACTORY

This was one of the earlier cases we saw, and illustrates the extreme derivative pricing that was going on at the time.

A family business run by father and sons in the volume retail sector, borrowed £2.2 million over 20 years, amortising over the last 15 years to buy property, and were sold a 15-year derivative in September 2007. The derivative rate was 5.5%, and Base rate was 5.75% at the date of sale. Sounds a good deal?

September 2007 was around the time of the Northern Rock crisis. This was a particularly good month for selling derivatives to SMEs – highly profitable products could look superficially attractive.

On the face of it, that sounds a good deal, but the industry standard pricing, reveals a value of initial client benefit of £2,000, and of initial client detriment of £144,000.

In the recent "Plevin" legal case, a contract which paid out 71.8% of premium as commission was investigated. The Supreme Court said that this should have been disclosed. We can therefore assume 28.2% might have represented benefit value, but this could have been lower, due to other expenses.

The above ratio is 1.4% of benefit (say - £2000/(£144,000-£2,000)) and 98.6% of "other" – which is not just commission, but represents the value of customer detriment.

Now, it should be noted that this was a commercial transaction, and so is not covered by consumer legislation. However, describing this contract as

"Hedging", "Insurance", or "Protection", stretches the English language, in my view, far beyond its limitations.

As a cash flow hedge, this deal left a lot to be desired, although the contract was designed so that the early months looked good. When interest rates fell from 5.75% to 0.5%, the payments needed for swap and loan actually went up by about 20%! This, again, is due to the fact that, when interest rates fall, loan repayments do not change as much as you might expect, due to capital repayments (see the Preface); also whereas derivative payments are not geared; accordingly, if rates rise, you get the full increase, and if they fall, you get the full hit. The element of cash flow hedging is therefore limited. Setting up a spreadsheet to show this is a simple matter for any accountant.

When the client complained, the bank initially did something rather clever. They pretended to capitalise the higher derivative payments into notional loan repayments, then extended the term of the new 'loan'. This reduced the regular payments, but effectively created a higher loan, which was then to be serviced at an annual fixed cost. I spent a long time staring at this with Carl to try and understand what had actually been done – it was Carl that finally "got it". It would be fascinating to compare what the client was actually told, with how this new arrangement was shown on the bank's books.

As an extra twist to the story, Barclays actually put the derivative in the personal names of the Cantors. Whether this was simply a cock-up, or the salesman thought he was being clever we don't know. (There is a fair stream of bank incompetence running through some of these cases). Barclays then tried very hard to persuade them to change the swaps to be in the company name, citing all sorts of reasons, (to avoid COB/COBS rules, I suspect) but the family had got wise by this time, and refused.

Collateralisation issues make the detriment *far* worse than £144,000. There was also a second swap, where the net profit was a mere £48,000 on a £1.25 million loan (the £48,000 is made up of £6,000 benefit and £54,000 detriment).

The graph overleaf shows the picture, for both swaps combined. At the worst point, December 2008, the swaps represented an immediate debt of over £1 million. That is the amount required to break the contract. However, including the collateralisation (the amount any bank would need to reserve to cover the possible debt), the worst point is around £1.8 million.

Even with the weaknesses in the FCA review, such an extreme case could not be ignored. The upshot was a successful compensation claim via the FCA review. Not all victims were so fortunate.

I cover later how such a contract would be seen within a GRG/BSU type banking unit, post the 2008 crash.

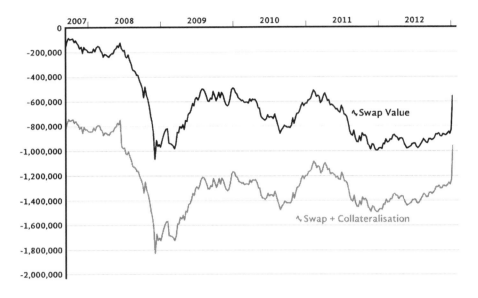

2.
HOW THE BANKS SAW IT

Father Brown got to his feet, putting his hands behind him. 'Odd, isn't it,' he said, 'that a thief and a vagabond should repent, when so many who are rich and secure remain hard and frivolous, and without fruit for God or man?

G.K. Chesterton Brown – The Innocence of Father Brown

First, when I talk about a bank, I emphasise that what I say does not apply to all the staff. The girls (and boys) behind the counter are clearly not involved directly in planning any sophisticated mis-selling processes. They clearly would not understand the first thing about derivatives. As you move further up the food chain, the position changes with regard to expected behaviour and 'loyalty', but not necessarily with regard to perception or understanding of what is really going on. The bank's branch managers (or "Relationship Managers", as they became) would be encouraged to promote 'hedging', and drop hints about risk; but they would not really understand exactly what skullduggery was actually being carried out.

Ignorance of the risks and nature of the derivatives sold extended to relatively senior ranks within the banks. *Seniority was no guarantee of awareness of risk.* This is illustrated by the fact that certainly the vast majority of senior executives in banks have high levels of integrity. They would not have knowingly sanctioned such behaviours. Those senior ranks would have been fed a sanitised version of events, and having merely perceived that sales processes were profitable, would have mentally moved on. They would not be spending too much time wondering why such contracts were suddenly being sold, or how the substantial profits it generated were made.

However, there is a natural human tendency to not want to be made to look ridiculous. If one's colleagues and subordinates tacitly approve of something; there is a disinclination to investigate too closely, if things appear to be running smoothly, lest one be thought a fool. Or, sometimes, to even investigate after a serious crisis. To quote Mark Twain, "It's easier to fool people than to convince them that they have been fooled."

For example, see National Australia Bank's 2004 Report and Accounts – the shortened version contains the following:

"The Board has undergone significant transformation during the past year, following the commitment of the Chairman for fundamental Board renewal in the wake of the foreign currency options trading losses incurred by the National. By the end of December 2004, six new, non-executive Directors and two additional executive Directors will have joined the Board, with another six Directors retiring or resigning during the year. The Board now has an extensive balance of skills and experience, with diversity across industries,

geographies, backgrounds and cultures. For details of the Board renewal program, see page 8 of this report.

Page 8 can wait for another day. But just look at how many got the boot! Do
you think any of the six ousted directors actually understood exactly what was
going on? My betting would respectfully be that they are unlikely to understand it *even now*.

You therefore have a group of individuals - you could think of them as 'the
meat in the sandwich'. These individuals are at the middle/senior management level, - although some may not have line management responsibilities -
who know what behaviour generates profit, and may be willing to take
excessive risk to boost the bank's, and their personal profits. In short, you
could think of a bank like a cake. The cherries on top impresses you. The
icing sugar coating is the cheap covering. But inside, who knows?

Others at the bank may not object if:

a) they really do not understand, or can dissimulate to the effect that they
    don't
b) are discouraged from asking questions, and
c) receive a share of the spoils.

The overall position is not dissimilar to that created by Nick Leeson at
Barings. Profits were generated by means not immediately understandable to
the line management of the bank – even at senior level. Leeson therefore
achieved 'cult status', due to the apparently risk-free profits that he generated
for Barings. It was not realised that he was exposing the bank to substantial
risk, and to what degree, until it was too late.

The key moment was when Leeson exposed the bank to a 'short straddle'.
In essence this was a bet that the values of certain assets would *not* move too
much. If those asset values stayed within a certain range, he would make a
profit. On the other hand, unexpected movements either way would hit him
hard. He was betting that these movements did not happen. In effect, he was
insuring the market himself.

The Kobe earthquake put paid to that game. Leeson's trading losses ballooned from £200m at the end of 1994 to £800m on 23 February 1995. That

was twice Barings' available capital. Leeson had managed to bust the bank over a period just less than two months.

Whereas it is a pretty safe bet that no-one in Barings apart from Nick Leeson (and perhaps a few of his associates) really knew what was going on until the train hit the buffers, there were whole departments instigating and managing derivative dealing. In principle, banks, including Barings, understood the theory explaining what a 'Rogue Trader' could achieve. Such potential problem traders were supervised by dedicated compliance departments. It was, as far as the bank was concerned, a very organised process. However, Leeson did not find it difficult to use the bank's "88888" account (an account used to correct errors), to hide his losses. 8 is considered lucky by the Chinese.

When considering derivative selling (or mis-selling), the key department of the bank to look at is generally called Treasury, Treasury Advisory, or something similar. (The latter is a strange title, bearing in mind that the structure of some of the sales jobs involved heavily promoting a product range, while using legalistic clauses within the product contracts to deny that 'advice' had been given.) Apart from them, very few people at the banks understand derivatives, or derivative risk.

There was certainly no-one in any bank accused of mis-selling who had both the understanding of what was being done, and the morality to effectively object to it. Any objections would have been swept aside, as the profit (or, at least, apparent profit), booked by the operation was too attractive to forego – especially as other banks were doing it. To forego such a profit source would not have been practically possible.

The salesmen and women were therefore presented with a choice – either continue to sell the products (with volume-based commissions), despite any qualms; or leave- possibly to worse paid jobs within the same bank. As many salesmen and those carrying out related activities were on substantial commission-based salaries – in most cases significantly in excess of the regionally based branch staff with whom they dealt; a major cut in pay would clearly have been unappetising.

While the swap selling process was exposing the clients to risk, it was also exposing the banks to a different sort of risk. Banks were employing senior subsidiary boards with such titles as 'Group Risk Committee', but they clearly missed both their banks' clients and their own banks' danger, by effectively endorsing the practices we have seen.

The banks were aware that their world was changing. Commercial borrowers were becoming more financially aware; and realising that the old world of using the executive lunch, and other jollies, to generate much larger profits was no longer working. Borrowers were capable of, and did, treat banks and their products more as commodity providers. This was partly a consequence of the banks' own behaviour. The new RBS model with emphasis on profitable sales from all aspects of the business, combined with ruthless cost cutting; had meant that loan underwriting had become a more and more centralised process. The local branch managers were put under greater and greater pressure to generate sales and profits. However, they were not capable of dealing with derivatives, due to the technical nature and riskiness of these product sales. This is why the specialist salesmen were employed and supervised separately. The relationship with the branch manager was geared towards building up to the 'quick hit' from the swap salesman. Relationship banking, in its real sense, went out of the window. The traditional avuncular figure, available frequently to provide advice and caution, was turned into a commission-hungry salesman.

The centralisation of decision making by banks was partly motivated by the general increase in the practice of securitisation of loans and mortgages. Formerly, the main client was the retail customer, and the products would be designed to generate profit; while the underwriting would ensure that poor risks were adequately loaded for, or excluded. If the bank changed its focus from professionally underwriting loans to what collateralised bunches of those loans it could sell on, the process became simpler (at least superficially). Individual underwriting could be relaxed, as loans were grouped together and sold on in tranches, with a wide variety of 'slicing' of income and capital repayments. Misleading credit ratings persuaded wholesale buyers that the security of these 'packages' was far greater than the reality showed. When the music stopped (first time round) in the UK, Northern Rock was the first major casualty.

As far as the SME market was concerned, derivatives also offered the advantage that much of the product downside could be hidden in the sales process. Whereas loans, (the products that the SMEs sought in the first place) were relatively simple for them to master, (I am leaving fixed interest rate loans out of this discussion for the moment); derivatives could generate profits in a way that was effectively concealed from the purchaser.

Moreover, banks were well versed in dealing with derivatives. They employed specialist teams to trade in units of tens or hundreds of millions of pounds; and successful traders could generate substantial profits for the bank from this. However, exposing large amounts of capital meant that significant losses were also on the cards; the traders had to be both astute and experienced.

The product ranges that were sold were also interesting. Most of the SME derivative sales were swaps, where the buyer commits to paying a fixed rate and receives a floating rate for the term of the contract. Margins for selling these could be substantial – far greater than the trader would earn by selling swaps in the market – and far greater than could be justified by arguing that retail overheads would be higher than for wholesale trading in large amounts. The reason for this is - that while the usual market counterparty would be well aware of the current market rates, and call out any trader who tried to overprice; SME's could be easily deceived that a rate offered was a good one, or that the market was moving against them, and it was important not to delay. Hence the "you need to buy now" line.

The cash mechanics of the products were, however, easier to understand (as opposed to their financial significance, which was not). To be able offer a range of products, variants of the straight swap were introduced. Since the development of Black Scholes techniques (named after two US professors) in the 1970s, it had become possible to value (or "price" to use the industry jargon) these "barrier" options (i.e., caps and floors); and pricing techniques were generally agreed by the swaps market. To illustrate this, if any derivative is specified adequately (the ISDA agreement uses standardised terms to describe these), any trader in that market can put a price on it; and traders will generally agree, with some latitude, what that price is. The process involved is data-hungry, investigating rates for all related trades over, say, the previous ninety days. This is done in practice using a "Bloomberg" or similar market information system.

Due to the substantial volumes of derivatives held by banks, regulators insisted that pricing for reporting purposes was primarily carried out on a market value basis (using the traders' terminology, the instruments were 'marked to market' – accountants would say 'fair value').

The simplest variant was the "collar" – rather than paying a fixed rate, the SME would pay a variable rate; but this was always above or equal to a specified rate (the 'floor'), and below or equal to a higher specified rate (the 'cap'). The combination of a cap and a floor into a single contract was called a collar.

Both swaps and collars were, common products in the derivatives markets, however, the volumes of swap in existence were, and are, far greater. However, what was not common was the other variant shown in the literature – generally known as a 'structured collar'. These had substantial penalties imposed if the interest rate (usually base rate) fell below a certain point. The rate charged might then be augmented by adding the degree to which the rate had fallen below the floor; or having a 'knock in' rate. If the rate fell below a certain level, a higher fixed rate was then payable. The products therefore had a level of what appeared to be technical credibility, in that a benefit was provided; but the mechanics disguised the fact that the actual goal was to expose the borrower to downside interest rate risk, and, most importantly, market risk. (This term is defined, together with those terms for other Basel II risks, below).

Products were often presented in packs of three – swap, collar, and structured collar; and the more complex/structured products were promoted on the basis of the cap rate being generally lower than that for a straightforward collar – but this was misleading. The pessimistic outlook of the market meant that a 1/4% rise in the level of the cap was insignificant in value; compared to a 1/4% rise in the level of the floor. However, this was not apparent from the sales presentations, which restricted themselves to historic views of interest rates. Where the forward curve was shown, (rarely, it appears), its real significance was not discussed.

What is also interesting is how financial conditions at any point in time (and timing is essential to this process), determine what products can be attractive (to the buyer) and profitable at the same time. For example, in October 2007 it was possible to sell profitable swaps where the entry rate was lower than current base rate. These would have been the happiest times for the salesmen. On the other hand, about six months earlier, the same swap (profit wise) would have cost more, and the salesman would then have had to emphasise his range of collars, or, in extremis, structured collars.

BANKING HOTHOUSE

I have referred to the collective group that designed and managed the process of mis-selling, or selling derivatives to the SME sector as "the hothouse". This phrase encapsulates both the quality of their intellects, and they pressure they were under in order to generate profits. They would have been well rewarded for good 0performance- but underachievement would not have been tolerated – and the worst aspects of sales team management would have been applied to those unfortunates.

Basically, there were two direct roles to the (miss) selling – pricing and selling. Despite the knowledgeable image that the salesmen attempted to portray (and some still do), they were, on the whole, ignorant of the full range of risks that these products entailed. They would, however, have been well advised on all of the benefits to trumpet before they were let loose on clients. The real knowledge worker was, in fact, the trader (or "pricer"). This was the individual who would have been buying and selling swaps in the market to support the salesman. As the market was liable to change – sometimes rapidly (but often did not move at all), the products needed to be kept up to date. Moreover, changes in the shape of the yield curve meant that different products would have to be presented at different times; the goals were profit, and early income flows of either zero or relatively small amounts in the clients' favour. In that way, the risks could be more easily concealed, and for longer – which is the essence of mis-selling.

THREE PARTS OF THE PRESENTATION

The PowerPoint Slide presentations so beloved of the swaps salesmen consisted of three parts:

1) The first was an introductory section, naming the individuals involved in selling, their titles, and department titles. Often, recent awards were cited as well; (see Nick Dunbar's "The Devil's Derivatives" for an amusing de-

scription of how these awards and the award ceremonies were developed). A selective history of UK Base Rate often followed, pointing out certain highs and lows, and attributing causes. (The actual economic reasons for high or low rates were not considered worthy of mention).

2) The "Pack of Three" products followed, and perhaps then a summary slide of the three, citing pros and cons. I was amused to note that the same mistake in describing Structured Collars appeared in more than one presentation. Clearly, the banks were better at cut and paste than they were at peer review! Although the error mis-described the product by 100%, it may or may not have helped in a claim against the bank, depending on how the judge viewed it.

3) Finally, came the small print – a pack of legal exclusions (described by lawyers as either basis clauses or exclusion clauses – most people would see them as get-out clauses), claiming absolution from any misleading statements that the bank made; and claiming that the swap contract was separate from the loan. This was not true, as the two were unavoidably interlinked.

Swap mis-selling first came about in the UK in the late 1980s, when local authorities, most notably Hammersmith and Fulham, speculated up to, and beyond, the hilt, in betting that interest rates would fall. After a struggle, they were largely bailed out by a high court ruling, which stated that Councils could not indulge in financial speculation, and that all derivatives sold fell into this category. An excellent description can be found in Duncan Campbell-Smith's book "Follow the Money" – the chapter "Closing the Swap Shop", merits reading and rereading several times. I expand on "Hammersmith" in Chapter 12.

The most recent spate of mis-selling (roughly 2005 – 2009, although there is evidence that some banks bounced their clients into derivative based products earlier than this) was developed, in my view, by Barclays Bank, under the leadership of Bob Diamond. I have based this judgement on the book F.I.A.S.C.O, written by Professor Frank Partnoy – which describes the product angles, the selling techniques and the get-out clauses, in such detail that I have no doubt that Partnoy's former employing banks were masters of such deceptive processes. Partnoy worked for First Boston, then Morgan Stanley. Bob Diamond worked for Morgan Stanley… and then First Boston. In addition, Nick Dunbar's book, The Devil's Derivatives, pages 68-71, describes discussions between Bob Diamond and his derivatives star trader, Oka Usi. If any Barclays (or other bank) staff have evidence to the contrary, I will be happy to amend this assertion.

Whoever "invented" this sales process, it cannot be denied that RBS were kings of the jungle as regards volume. In the initial FSA assessment, their sales by number almost added to the sum of the other three major banks added together!

Well Done, Fred!

MAIN OBJECTIONS
The main objection to bank derivative sales to SMEs is that banks presented risk as 'hedging'

I have discussed the sales and reviewed the documents for over 80 victims of this mis-selling. The vast majority of the derivatives I have seen miss-sold involve a misleading sales script - this misleads by omission. The technical term for the process is "misleading synecdoche", which I will expand on later in the book. It is perhaps better understood as mixing up financial poison and financial vitamins; then describing the mixture as "vitamins"; and then describing some, but not all, of the downsides of the poison. I can provide financial justification for all of the above.

The most startling thing to emerge from all this dubious practice, is that EU Banking Regulators, under the Basel II rules, described four basic categorisations of risks. What banks then did, in essence, was to wrap up those risks, as defined, and sell them on as "hedging". Effectively, someone at the bank said "If these are risks, and identified as such within bank regulation, then the opposite is a benefit. If we can create those risks in the derivatives market, and persuade SME's to shoulder them, then we can then profitably sell on the other side of the deal."

BASEL II RISK CATEGORISATIONS

I have taken my risk definitions from "Risk Management and Shareholder Value in Banking", by Andrea Resti and Andrea Seroni, 2007 edition. This provides a clear exposition of risks and regulation at the time of the mis-selling (2005 – 2009).

The four main risks can be denoted as follows:

1) Interest Rate (Cash Flow) Risk
2) Market Risk
3) Credit Risk
4) Operational Risk

As the expression "Interest Rate Risk" is ambiguous, I have referred to it as cash flow risk. For a bank, the two are similar, as most of its cash flow risk relates to interest charged and received. However, for a trading company, or individual, a substantial amount of their cash flow is likely to come from other sources. The term "Interest Rate Risk" can also be easily used to mislead others.

1) **Cash Flow Risk** is then, in short, the risk of not being able to pay your bills. It is clearly an acute risk – immediate action is required. It is, in fact, so acute that it could be described as the crystallisation of financial risk, rather than the risk itself. If this happens to you, you are in big trouble. If this happens to a bank, it is in even bigger trouble.

2) **Market Risk** is the risk of falls in asset values. For example, if you own a house outright, and property values fall by 10%, you experience a 10% reduction in the portion of your wealth that the house represents. In other words, you are, in reality, poorer. However, the inconvenience is only acute if you have to sell the house now. If you can wait, any general rise in property prices may well wipe out your losses, if house prices rise by more than 10%. This risk is then chronic, not acute.

3) **Credit Risk** is a risk that banks are exposed to, not borrowers[1]. Imagine that a bank makes mortgage loans to ten identical homebuyers. One month later, one buyer is told he has lost his job. Clearly, his immediately ability to make his monthly repayments is lower. The advent of risks of this nature is called credit risk.

4) **Operational Risk** is, basically, every other risk. Operational risks affect all businesses, and can be broadly divided in two – statistical risk and "enemy action". Statistical risk includes such areas as computers breaking down, floods, etc.; while enemy action encompasses both internal and external fraud. Steps can be taken to protect against both of these types of operational risk.

For financial organisations, the first three risks are the most important, and they are often mixed up – sometimes deliberately. That was a main cause of the 2008 financial crisis.

Banks also suffer public "credit events", that of Allied Irish Bank in June 2011 being notable.[2]

Those three main risks can usefully be analysed in terms of you making a house purchase. Cash flow risk is manifested when you don't have the money to make your monthly payment. Market risk is the risk of negative equity. Credit risk is the lender's, (not your), risk, due to *some* loans going bad.

The great error which induced the crash was the assumption, that by "slicing and dicing", you could get rid of MARKET risk, as well as credit risk. If a lender collateralises, and sells on, a tranche of loans, then if one loan goes sour, its effect on the receiving party is reduced, as the risk effect is spread over a number of borrowers, who do not also suffer in the same way. But with

---

[1] However, the queues outside Northern Rock in 2007 showed that investors thought that the bank was a "bad bet", and its credit risk was high, compared to that of other banks. As they believed this would precipitate into cash flow risk, they sought to be at the front of the queue for withdrawals, before the money ran out.

[2] http://www2.isda.org/news/isda-determinations-committee-allied-irish-banks-plc-failure-to-pay-credit-event

MARKET risk, the effect is universal – a property crash is likely to affect ALL properties; so the imagined "balancing out" of the risk just doesn't exist. Here are roundabouts, but no swings. Any derivative sold is essentially a chunk of negative equity at the point of sale, which could get better, but could also get worse. That is why other lenders turned down potential borrowers for refinance if they had a swap in their books.

FOURTEEN PARAGRAPHS COVERING SWAP MIS-SELLING

1) The growing realisation that traditional bank lending was unlikely to continue to generate the high profit margins it had done previously, added fuel to the fire. To the naïve, swaps represented a risk-free source of bank income.

2) A major bank asset was the perception that they (the bank) could be trusted as gatekeepers to borrowing, via their loan underwriting processes. If a bank was prepared to lend to you, you could consider yourself creditworthy on the strength of that decision. Moreover, if a bank offered you a term loan, you could expect that its underwriters had based their calculations on that loan running for the full term. Business loans are generally shorter term, than residential mortgages.

3) Such trust has now disappeared in the wake of banks' behaviour utilising units such as GRG, BSUs, West Register, Isobel and Cerberus. Their trust asset has been squandered.

4) A "race to the bottom", whereby if an unsavoury practice was adopted by one market participant, and the regulator did not (perhaps could not) object; then the rest if the market would follow suit. This explains why pension mis-selling was an industry-wide phenomenon (after Prudential's lead); and swap mis-selling generally took off after Barclay and RBS' lead.

5) The backstop position that clients' asset bases would protect the banks if "things went wrong". As loan covenants were far-reaching, a bank could

generally find some breach, however minor, and exploit it (or, failing that, engineer it), in the case of interest rates falling too severely. In the event, those asset bases were utilised to recapitalise the banks in greatest distress, especially for RBS.

6) Some clients reported breeches of bank covenants, and were astounded to find that the bank jut took advantage of this. For an example, see Neil Mitchell's "Torex" story. Mitchell discovered fraudsters in his company, and reported it to the police – and RBS – who promptly shut down his business. Moral – if you borrow from RBS, keep your mouth shut on crime!

7) Exclusion clauses could absolve the bank from liability, if they had made misleading statements in connection with the swap sale. In particular, they could exclude mention of the fact that the derivative might form part of a breach of loan covenants. The nature of swaps obviously made refinancing the loan difficult, if not impossible. Not only due to the extra risk, but it also meant another bank had snaffled the profit on the swap, so the opportunity for the new bank was gone!

8) A similar excuse was used in pension mis-selling, where the existence of an existing company group scheme was countered with the comment that: "we are not allowed to advise on company schemes". The sale of a product which required exit from a better scheme was therefore justified by the "Non-advice" argument. Using the blanket term "hedging" in a misleading context, and stating that if the product was not understood, advice should be sought (this excuse being deemed to justify misleading sales statements and omissions) is a useful parallel.

9) Dedicated sales forces were fuelled by commission remuneration, and gaudy "production gimmicks":– ringing a bell in the office when a sale is made, so everyone can hear it - bottles of champagne as sales rewards, etc. Descriptions of the RBS sales environment, where the loans department had a large sign on the wall, saying "No swap – no loan" – typified the processes. With some RBS cases, the trick was to promise the loan, sell the swap – and then withdraw the loan offer!

10) Selling and promoting these products involved high costs in the following areas:

- Recruitment
- Training
- Motivation
- Supervision
- Compliance
- Remuneration
- Disciplinary
- Decruitment

11) The salesmen and saleswomen in the teams also needed to work hard and effectively to justify all of these costs; also they needed to be able to sell, whatever external financial conditions looked like.

12) The FCA/FSA's "CF30" qualification was deemed adequate to allow the products to be sold without mention of market risk, or collateralisation. Notably, ISDA's standard Credit Support Annex, which describes the concealed risks, appears to never have been used. Commission-based salesmen selling life assurance products and pensions had been generally banned by the FSA for rule infringements. It was as if those same salesmen simply took their CF30 qualifications to banks, and started doing interest rate swap sales instead.

13) Sales promotion slides were generally in three sections – after a "Credentials" opening, some interest rate history was presented, implying that variable interest rates were a factor to be worried about. Three products were then explained, each being a "derivative with downside", (or "DWD" as distinct from a cap, which has no ambiguous downside) – often a straight swap, collar, or "structured collar". The exclusion clauses described above completed the package.

The presentations are covered in more detail above.

14) The regulator at the time, the FSA, was powerless, or deemed itself powerless, to challenge banks' sales processes. Any interference in bank activities

was scotched with Tony Blair's "Red Tape" speech in June 2005 –which led to the following riposte - "FSA blasts Blair for 'damaging' speech"[3]

Despite the massive criticism that the FSA took, it is clear that, if you are a regulator, and if the government briefs against you, you have an uphill struggle to "do the right thing".

However, the FSA did seem to manage to restrict banks to a profit/commission cap of 20 basis points (bps) per year of term x notional agreed between banks and FSA. A basis point is 1/100 of 1% - so 20 basis points equals 0.2%. This may seem tiny – but it needs to be seen in context of the likely payment costs – not the loan itself. The failings in this method are covered later, but, given the circumstances, it is a wonder the FSA even managed that!

It is clearly true that sales to SMEs are (and not unreasonably) less controlled and regulated than those to private individuals – in the commercial world, it is appropriate to expect a greater degree of self-responsibility in commercial dealings. However, each party has a duty, even if not strictly in law, not to mislead, even if the misleading is carried out by omission.

1) Bank traders in the swaps market would assess the market, and trade on behalf of the bank, thus the dealing system would pit "expert against expert". However, with SME sales, the banks were selling into a market totally unaware of either market prices, or relative risks. The "20 basis points" rule described above was certainly not universally observed, and, as seen in the example in the previous chapter, a coach and horses could be driven through it.

2) Bank branch managers (now titled "Relationship Managers", or "RMs"), were incentivised, both via carrot and stick, to support swap salesmen, by hinting that 'interest rates were something to be concerned about'. The same individuals were expected to placate angry clients when things had gone wrong, and the salesman was nowhere to be found.

3) A bank was not seen, by its staff "in the know" as an institution which

---

[3] http://www.telegraph.co.uk/finance/2916849/FSA-blasts-Blair-for-damaging-speech.htmlBlair bank bombshell

required integrity in any of its methods or practices, apart from vacuous "mission statements" and the like.

4) The process not surprisingly, degenerated into an increasing cycle of chicanery, where positive market movements gave the opportunity for an "upsell", and more and more risk was stuffed into the unknowing clients' balance sheets.

5) To cover themselves against undue credit exposure on rate falls, banks planned to use the techniques so well described by Roger Lane-Smith in his autobiography "A Fork in the Road", exploiting the derivative lock-in and credit detriment. The "Special Situations" units he describes so well were actually called into action in order to recapitalise the banks, especially RBS's notorious GRG and West Register operations.

The next chapter investigates the aggregate effect of swap sales on the financial strength and resilience of SMEs. This covers the group of SMEs as a whole – how attractive (or otherwise) they became to lenders, and how the pressured sale of derivatives "uprisked" the sector and its members, like termites burrowing into the fabric of a building but leaving the outer shell intact. So, although apparently solid, it will collapse under the slightest.

EXAMPLE
GREEN AND ROWLEY – ROYAL BANK OF SCOTLAND ("RBS")

Messrs Green and Paul Rowley, two gentlemen involved in the restaurant business, borrowed money (in respect of property purchase) from RBS. They were sold a derivative by Mrs Kay Gill and Mrs Karen Holdsworth, who specialised in the arrangement of interest rate management products for RBS.[4]

The swap, issued on 25 May 2005, had a 10-year term, and was issued at a rate of 4.83%. Both the original judgment by His Honour of Judge Waksman QC, and the appeal judgement of Lord Justice Tomlinson, Lady Justice Hallett, and Lord Justice Richards, comment that this was "only fractionally

---

[4] This is from the Court of Appeal report

http://www.bailii.org/ew/cases/EWCA/Civ/2013/1197.html

more than 4.75%", which was Base Rate at that time, on which the loan interest was based. To a derivative specialist, this is a red herring. The significance of a derivative is its capital value, which will depend on the shape of the forward curve at the pricing date. The current base rate is only one element of that pricing. It is like the opening five minutes of a football match – it might be a good guide to the final result – or it may not.

To show the significance of the 0.08% difference, I have provided a graph which shows how a derivative would have been priced on 25 May 2005. This differs from the previous graphs, as it is all about "day 1" – the view of the next ten years of the future as at 25 May 2005: this is shown on the next page.

The black line is the curve (unsmoothed) showing where the market is trading future interest rates. Note also the dark grey line, at 4.75%, the lower the black line is below the dark grey line, the more profitable that part of the swap is for the bank.

Now, the bank can take its profit from all of the area between the black and dark grey lines on the day the swap is issued.

Now look at the lighter grey line. This is set in order to be *totally above* the black line.

So by setting the rate at 4.83%, RBS ensures maximum profitability – and the pricing is such that the value of the benefits to the client, (as valued in the multi-trillion derivatives market, which *the FSA* also considered appropriate for banks to formally value derivatives) was nil.

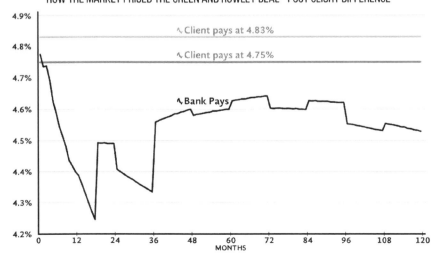

HOW THE MARKET PRICED THE GREEN AND ROWLEY DEAL - POST SLIGHT DIFFERENCE

Black line - where the market is trading future interest rates.
Dark grey line - there would have been some, albeit minimal, value to Green and Rowley.
Now look at the light grey line. This is set in order to be *totally above* the black line. No value to client.

This is profiteering taken to the extreme. However, whether it is illegal is another matter. Profiteering is not racketeering.

The surprise of both Mrs Gill and Messrs Green and Rowley that the break cost of the swap was some £139,000 would not have been reflected in the attitude of someone who regularly priced derivatives. What is more, the detriment was not limited to the level of £139,000, and the pain could not necessarily be lessened by spreading it over the following six years. This is due to collateralisation issues, which are covered later. Suffice it to say, any business with such an unpredictable security in its books would have been a highly unattractive prospect for any alternative lender with whom Messrs Green and Rowley might have tried to refinance.

However, you do now understand what RBS means when it uses the term "hedging"!

The court reports in this case are all in the public domain.

3.
HOW THE MARKET SAW IT

"I mean that we here are on the wrong side of the tapestry,' answered Father Brown. 'The things that happen here do not seem to mean anything; they mean something somewhere else. Somewhere else retribution will come on the real offender. Here it often seems to fall on the wrong person."

G.K. Chesterton - The Innocence of Father Brown

Reviewing the position of SMEs as a whole, the quality of this market sector as a lending proposition deteriorated due to swap sales.

Derivative sales to SMEs by banks, in connection with term loans, increased significantly from around the year 2000 through to 2009; at which point the market and interest rates collapsed and the detriment embodied in the products became apparent. In brief, the products sold, or mis-sold, over this period, had the effect of diminishing the value of assets held by SME's as a group. The net beneficiaries were those who bought the other sides of these trades in the market. These would have included large pension schemes, the Pension Protection Fund, and anyone else who was either covering their downside risks, or speculating on interest rates falling.

The effective withdrawal of SME capital at the end of that period slowed down UK recovery, extending the length of the recession. Not only did SME entrepreneurs lack the funds to expand their businesses and develop new ones, they no longer trusted the banks who had put them in this position. Loan finance was regarded with suspicion, especially if accompanied by hard sell promotions, such as swaps, or pushing for fixed rates, (as opposed to variable rate), loans. Interest rates, as assessed by Bank Base Rate, have languished at ½% (or lower) since 2009, and the forward interest rate curve has flattened since then, indicating that pessimism has been increasing.

New providers have entered the market, such as Metrobank, who only lend from their own funds; and crowdfunding lenders such as Funding Circle, who raise capital from their website and post details of borrowers and their borrowing needs on there. However, these will take longer to expand into the UK economy, and replace the other dishonest lenders effectively.

Virtually all derivative sales degraded the borrower's covenant vis a vis market risk (defined briefly in chapter 2, and more fully later).

The fundamental damage done by derivative sales was generated by market risk. When a company borrows funds, the lender usually insists on a set of income and capital covenants. The capital covenants are usually administered less rigorously than income ones; (the most important covenant being the requirement that interest and capital repayments are made as agreed i.e. non-default).

Derivatives were sold as if they were a simple arrangement, involving exchanges of cash at predetermined future points in time. In practice, they each have a capital value that is more sharply and formally defined than for loans.

The actual SME loans are not traded, either on a recognised exchange or on an ad hoc basis (i.e., known as "over the counter"). That is, unless the bank gets into trouble. Then it wreaks harm on its loan clients, then sells them off in bulk to an external processing unit; such as the infamous Cerberus, which most UK businesses would no more go near than borrowing from the Kray twins. However, derivatives are very different – a major quality is their market value, which fluctuates, sometimes violently. Hook your company into derivatives – and that debt is public knowledge – quoted on Bloomberg, for all to see.

Derivatives are, by design, highly flexible in their creation; (although, once the terms are agreed, each party is rigidly locked into them.) Accordingly, unless the participants have the financial credibility (as measured by net assets or income) of a major institution, collateralisation arrangements need to be made to ensure that the ensuing contract commitments can be met. These may change as the derivative risk becomes greater or smaller; or they may change between the parties as financial conditions change over time.

A stronger party contracting into a derivative with a weaker party, would be likely to want to specify precisely collateral arrangements. The standard tool for this, developed by ISDA (the same body that devised the swap contracts), is called a Credit Support Annex (CSA). In a very interesting lecture a couple of years ago, two swap salesmen from RBS explained to an actuarial convention how these had been around since the 1990's. This was supported by information from independent advisors, such as Redington.

To my knowledge, not one mis-sold swap was sold in conjunction with a Credit Support Annex, nor was its absence explained at point of sale to any borrower. If they had, swap mis-selling would probably not have occurred – but then most of the derivative sales would not have taken place, either.

To make things worse, the borrowers were relying on their accounts, as verified by annual audits, to manage their businesses.

For smaller companies, where corporate financial support usually came from their accountant, derivatives would be an enigma. On the one hand, guidance stated that they should go into the balance sheet at their 'fair value' (or market value). On the other hand, they had been sold by a bank as 'hedging' for a loan, and business proprietors had been led to believe this. No market value was ever specified in sales literature – the only capital issue mentioned was that a break cost might be payable if the contract was exited early. This might be considered as similar to life assurance, where early surrender might involve a penalty, in that all premiums paid would not be returned on encashment in the early years of the contract. Derivative salesmen also used the terms 'insurance' and 'protection' copiously.

For business proprietors and their staff, it would seem unlikely that there would be a need to recognise a 'hedging' contract in the balance sheet if there was a corresponding loan it was 'hedging', or 'protecting'.

It also appears that auditors may have assumed in a number of cases that the adequately prudent course of action would have been to recognise the loan capital fully, and assumed that by ignoring the derivative value; they were being prudent (i.e., by not 'hedging' this capital value by reducing the loan). In fact, as the derivative had a negative value, this was not being prudent at all – and even now, banks see the derivatives as a greater risk than the market value assessment that auditors see as adequately prudent, even now.

In several cases, market values of derivatives were excluded from those accounts.

Accordingly, it was likely that capital values never turned up in the balance sheets of the holders. We have seen several incidences where this is the case.

Accounting rules state that 'hedges' should be classified as 'income hedges' or 'capital hedges'. I understand that if a derivative effectively converts a variable interest rate to a fixed one, it is then considered an 'income hedge'. This is interesting, since banks see fixed rates as riskier than variable rate ones. So, accountants and banks define risk in different ways; *and banks see this as an exploitable opportunity.*

I cannot see why any trading company should want to purchase a capital hedge, unless it related to a tax avoidance scheme, or suchlike. Moreover, the "Hedge Accounting" rules place great store on whether the company intends to hold the swap to maturity or not. What is not considered is that the swap may render the company insolvent long before this happens.

SMEs accordingly continued to manage their business using substantially uninformed monthly management accounts.

One factor I appreciated in investigating SMEs, and their financial abilities and methods, was that they paid a great deal of attention to cash flow, and monthly management accounts. They almost universally relied on the information from these monthly accounts to manage their businesses successfully. One client I met described these monthly accounts as his 'bible'. Clearly, any unexposed derivative risk would not show up in such accounts; so the business would, unbeknown to them, be running two sets of accounts.

Their ignorance made them an even worse risk to lenders.

The client's ignorance of the true state of affairs was a deterrent to any new lenders. The business becomes like a lorry driving in the fog, whose satnav tells him he is 50 meters from the edge of a cliff, whereas he is actually 5 meters away.

No-one put them in the picture, as those capable of doing so were all profiting from the same process.

Some new lenders tried to explain why they weren't lending, on account of this, but as many of them were in the game themselves, they didn't want to be too honest. For example, I heard one new bank say "that's the worst over-sale I've never seen". The speaker clearly had a blinkered view of what his own bank had been selling!

Other industry experts have been slow to address these problems, probably because the derivatives industry already has a bad name (see Warren Buffett et al), and they don't want to worsen it.

Effectively there was therefore nowhere that the client could receive honest advice as to what was going on. Accountants, including the SME's own auditor, just hadn't got it yet (and, judging by some of the verdicts they have provided as 'independent reviewers' under the FCA scheme, many still haven't).

The accounts that are produced in this respect could be described as "True and Fair to the Accountants – But Not Bankers" or "True and Fair – But Useless"

It does not take much imagination to see that this method of lending money must end in disaster. Businesses had been damaged by products gratuitously sold to them by misleading scripts and presentations, and commission driven hard-sell techniques. The derivative was the most uncontrollable aspect of the business, and, in ignorance of this, the owner was likely to make unwise decisions, and could then be blamed for any mistakes. Banks' "GRG" type units became masters of this.

Lehman Brother crashed in late 2008, leading to a credit crisis, which caused the UK base rate to be cut dramatically.

Swap mis-selling continued between the start of 2006, when the downward slope in the forward curve increased from the 2005 position; up until the end of 2008, when the dive in base rate not only reflected the drying up of lending, but also changed the economic conditions that made mis-selling possible.

Ironically enough, the market suffered a mini-crash towards the end of 2007, when, inter alia, the Northern Rock crisis hit the market. But false optimism throughout 2008 allowed derivative sales to continue through this time. Finally, with the full banking crisis being brought on by the demise of Lehman Brothers, together with the collapse of RBS and Lloyds TSB, the disaster was complete.

The fall in interest rates driven by Bank of England Monetary Policy Committee - inadvertently tipped those with FRLs and derivatives with downside (if, anything apart from a cap) into crisis.

The Bank of England Monetary Policy Committee manages interest rates in order to contain inflation and encourage growth. If the economy is booming, to the extent that overheating and inflation become real threats – they increase base rate, in order to dampen inflation. When the economy stumbles, and growth prospects subside, they cut the rate in order to stimulate growth.

Accordingly, "hedging" as provided by banks frustrates these aims - it works against what they are trying to do, and, when viewed holistically, is speculative. In a boom, the derivative provides unnecessary protection – in a slump, it generates unwanted exposure.

The view that the 2008/09 crash was a 'just bad luck' can be countered by three strong arguments:

When the 2008/09 crash did happen, many commentators were quick to describe it as a 'perfect storm' – 'an event the like of which could only occur once every 200 years', etc. This has been used as an excuse for selling products that caused the damage that derivatives did.

Those commentators conveniently ignore three things:

1)   In the UK, the failure of Northern Rock gave an indication of what might happen – the forward curve in late 2007 reverted to a panic alarm 'crisis' position. The warning was disregarded, as banks continued to push derivative sales through 2008.

     The unheeded warning meant that when Lehman Brothers, and many other financial institutions, crashed in Autumn 2008 (or, as Americans call it, the "Fall"), risk exposures were still high; and the crash was harder, deeper, and longer than it might have been otherwise.

2)   It would not have taken a base rate drop as severe as down to ½%, to cause the damage that the "hedging" derivatives caused.

3)   If a company borrowed £1,000,000 for 15 years at mid-2011, on a fixed rate interest only basis, its break cost by mid-2013 would have been £1,150,000 – up by around 15% - *even though base rate had stayed at ½% throughout the period. This gives the lie to the "bad luck" theory.*

Under the old accounting rules, companies would have shown that loan in the balance sheet at £1,000,000 throughout the term of the loan. Despite changed accounting regulations, it is still shown as £1,000,000. Now, if it were a "Variable Rate Loan Plus Swap", you would have to show it at £1,150,000. The CVA ("Credit Valuation Adjustment", or the extra risk margin I described earlier) is not allowed for in accounting for derivatives.

The next chapter explores how banks reacted when faced with squeezed margins within client loan books degraded by the swap sales. Post the 2008 crash, banks' speculative behaviour in derivatives had destroyed their capital bases, and huge bail-outs were required in some cases. However, these were not enough. Faced with regulators who now demanded they put their houses in order, and investors who shunned the sector, having been fooled before, banks resorted to squeezing their clients, often to and beyond the point of insolvency. For clients with swaps, this was easier – the swap rendered the client unattractive to other lenders, so he was trapped – the bank could then gouge their captive clients at will.

Large AMC's (Accountant/ Management Consultants - see the preface) were utilised to help, and shared in the spoils in many ways.

EXAMPLE
LIGNACITE – HSBC

Lignacite was an old established family company, run by descendants of the founder, who sold innovative materials to the building industry.

The company was sold a ten-year swap by HSBC in 2006 in conjunction with a factory refurbishment loan of some £4 million – there was no detailed slide show, but the salesman was clearly in regular contact with the company's finance director promoting various products and rates.

Reading the loan conditions, it is clear that the purchase of the derivative could have easily put Lignacite in breach of those conditions immediately, by exposing D to market and collateralisation risks. However, bank HSBC made no reference in its loan documentation as to how derivatives might be treated in respect of these covenants in future if, for example, interest rates fell.

On the other hand, the conditions also stated "If required by the Bank, the Borrower will enter into an interest rate hedging instrument satisfactory to the Bank at a level, for a period, and for a notional amount satisfactory to the Bank."

The bank also has the right to call in the loan immediately, subject to a number of conditions, one of which was:

> "any event which, in the opinion of the Bank (acting reasonably) gives grounds for belief that the Borrower might not perform its obligations under the Facility Letter".

What was in fact happening was that the bank was insisting on capital covenants, and then selling an instrument that would break those covenants if interest rates moved the wrong way. It is likely that the Bank was assuming it could use the clients' assets to securitise the derivative if rates fell, possibly applying a level of double counting to those assets (in its anxiety to achieve the day one derivative profit).

In HSBC's own 2004 accounts, it makes much of its concern regarding market risk. What it then does is wrap up some of this risk, and sell it on to the client as 'hedging'.

The swap proved disastrous for Lignacite. Post 2009, the bank forced the client into its "special support" unit, where it insisted on various measures, including overpriced invoice factoring, where the riskiest customers were excluded from the deal, and Lignacite was given no choice but to use HSBC's services.

Additional financial stress caused by the bank put the company under more severe pressure in the recession. A number of staff were made redundant, many who had served the company for many years, and whose new job prospects in a shattered economy would have been severely restricted.

The Bank has refused to enter into any meaningful negotiation, citing only that Lignacite had entered into the arrangement freely, and that interest rate cap prices had been quoted (although this does not justify under-describing the risks involved in an alternative swap product). Again, the risks to which Lignacite was exposed, exceeded the need to pay specific 'interest type' amounts at agreed future points in time; but capitalisation and collateralisation risks, that HSBC clearly thought it appropriate to describe as 'risk' when talking to shareholders, it was happy to describe as 'hedging' when selling for a day one profit.

In the graph overleaf, the black line is the value, and the grey line includes the collateralisation. The initial sale margin to the bank is £120,000. The total with collateralisation reaches a negative of about £820,000 at its worst points.

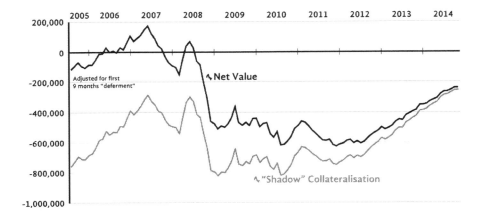

4.
HOW THE BANKS THEN SAW IT

He had killed, but not silenced. But his imperious intellect rose against the facer; there was one way yet. He could make the corpse less unaccountable. He could create a hill of corpses to cover this one. In twenty minutes eight hundred English soldiers were marching down to their death.

G.K. Chesterton – The Innocence of Father Brown

The banking world changed fundamentally in September 2009.

While the markets were still racing forwards, buoyed with increasingly irrational optimism, the swap game continued. Banks saw them as a source of easy profits: the salesman gains the borrowers trust, sells a product to up-risk him, takes the profit, and hopes nothing goes wrong. Or, if it does, the small print leaves the buyer carrying the can – and anticipating complaints, legal action; and the inevitable regulatory review. Plans were made to be able to defend behaviour retrospectively – we used get-out clauses – clients were told to take advice if they didn't understand the products; we weren't misleading anyone by using terms such as hedging, insurance, or protection – we didn't advise, or misadvise, etc.

On 8 October 2008, a bailout fund (Bank Recapitalisation Fund) was set up to recapitalise failing banks. The two banks worst hit were RBS and Lloyds TSB. Of them RBS were by far the hardest. The Royal Bank of Scotland Group raised £20 billion from the Bank Recapitalisation Fund; with £5 billion in preference shares and a further £15 billion being issued as ordinary shares. HBOS and Lloyds TSB together raised £17 billion; £8.5 billion in preference shares and a further £8.5 billion issue of ordinary shares.

Clearly, there were consequences. Just three days later, Sir Fred Goodwin was forced to retire from RBS, effectively to exit four months later, his post-Myners pension intact. Bob Diamond, Barclay's chief Executive, was forced out of office in July 2012. Although his departure centred around the bank's manipulation of LIBOR, Barclay's role in swap mis-selling had then become clear to regulators. The FSA announced its bank swap mis-selling review around this time, with the pilot scheme results being announced in March 2013.

Banks and their regulators now realised that the risks that they had been generating within the system were unsustainable. Banks had been effectively creating risk (as defined by Basel II), and stuffing it into borrowers' balance sheets; as well as the original risks tied to the loan covenants. When interest rates fell, the derivative debt ballooned in those SME borrowers' balance sheets. This drew attention to the "Credit Risk" to which banks had been exposed by the sales of the swaps, and which now had crystallised. The loans had become distressed, and, effectively, the swaps had distressed them, with crystallising market risk.

The regulators, freed from the restraints Gordon Brown and Tony Blair had placed on them, were asking awkward questions about capital adequacy and risk. Overnight, they went from "supine to vulpine", as an undercapitalised banking sector was seen as a dangerous national risk.

The government's secondary aim was to divest itself of its "toxic" bailout investments in RBS and Lloyds banks. The opposition demanded that the taxpayer received "value for money" for their bailout funds. Is this why the state controlled regulators were reluctant to criticise banks in anything but the vaguest terms? They now clearly have an agenda to "big up" the banking sector, given any chance they get.

Banks were, accordingly, under pressure to raise capital, to support, not only new borrowing, but their previous lending/swap packages. Barclays and HSBC had avoided taking funds from the government bail outs, but RBS and Lloyds were in the spotlight. However, the market was now fully aware of the quality of swap-blighted companies in terms of creditworthiness, as well as other bank misbehaviour; which seemed to be emerging on a weekly basis, often involving court action.

Looking at the legal position, insolvency law places cash driven breaches of covenants on a higher level of seriousness, than capital or other failings. The recent "Eurosail" court case is a good example of this. Accordingly, banks could not just bump borrowers into insolvency. The support of "GRG", "BSU", or similar named units was required, in order to batter clients into compliance and fight a war of attrition to filter off their liquidity, and acquire their assets.

As the swaps had destroyed the holders' creditworthiness, refinancing proved to be impossible. So as clients had usually allowed the same bank to manage all of their financial affairs, including control of their day to day bank accounts, they were effectively helpless. Clearly, if a bank can maintain that a covenant has been broken (to disagree meaning a legal battle against a far more powerful opponent), then unless a term loan can be repaid overnight (unlikely), the bank has the power to raise fees and charges without any constraint. Therefore, its de facto solvency or insolvency is totally in the hands of the bank.

To understand how banks operate, I now quote the opening passage from Chapter 31 – Banking from Roger Lane-Smith 's autobiography – "A Fork in the Road":

"A fairly certain way to grow a commercial law firm is to act for at least one major bank, and preferably two, three, or more."

"Banks are terrific clients, who produce a large amount of (normally) high quality legal work. They lend money (sometimes), and when they do, any significant loan needs to be documented, normally at the borrower's cost."

"If the loan runs into choppy waters, it normally moves into "intensive care", or whatever other soothing and helpful description ('business support') masks the true summary that the bankers in this section are hard as nails, charging their struggling clients substantial fees for advice, big fees for re-newed facilities (even if only short term) and if they have to move to administration then the bank's lawyers move in and sell off all the assets and/or 'restructure' the banking facilities."

"Many a great law firm has been built on a strong banking relationship".

With just these 150 – odd words, Mr Lane-Smith really says it all. No complaint from anyone who claims that their bank has gouged them could state the issues more eloquently, than this account from a man who, while clearly having profited substantially from supporting such banks and such behaviour, has not acted in any way inappropriately or unprofessionally.

This reinforces my short summary of the purpose of loan covenants in the documentation:

"If things go wrong, we'll take it back – or worse!"

Mr Lane-Smith goes on to describe his and his firm's relationships with those banks as follows:

"Within three to four years the Bank of Scotland was to become the largest client of the (his) firm in the UK, closely followed by Barclays and Royal Bank of Scotland. The Bank of Scotland' "integrated" finance division also became huge-ly successful and profitable for the bank. About five years after the inauguration dinner at Cameron House in Scotland, I was invited by Peter Cummins and Graeme (Shankland) to the celebration dinner held at The Grove near Watford. Again I gave the main after dinner speech, and everyone was in high spirits."

"The team were kings of the jungle!"

Clearly Mr Lane-Smith is not one for making unsubstantiated criticisms of banking – having been close to the industry, he tells it how it is. However, there is a difference in imposing harsh sanctions *when you have sold a product which causes the damage!*

Before we resort to all out criticism of banks for this behaviour, there are some points to be made in their defence:

1) Each bank, or even the group of all UK banks has a limited influence over the UK economy. What hit home in 2008 was a full-blooded bank crash – the world had changed.

2) In going from (relative) boom to sudden bust, the parameters on which each bank operated changed quickly. Up until 2008, easy lending was the norm; although the market had been given a warning in 2007, when Northern Rock (September 2007) had needed bailing out. Lehman Brothers' bankruptcy and the Bradford & Bingley bail-out (both September 2008) – changed the UK economy.

3) If reckless lending behaviour and risky swap selling are common practices in the industry, it is difficult for a participant to avoid them. With the threat of an acquisitive rival like RBS, who might stage a takeover at any time, banks needed to keep up, in terms of profit and growth.

4) Banks, quite properly, do need to protect themselves against loans "going bad" and regularly checked covenants are reasonable measures to impose. However, as long as repayments are made on time, it is generally regarded that other covenants, especially capital ones, are interpreted broadly. In other words, they are guide-lines, and not land-mines. Banks have clearly used aggressive interpretations of those covenants ("covenant-squatting"); in order to prosecute a strategy of replacing their solvency capital, by any means possible.

5) Under government pressure to lend more (Peter Mandelson's promise "We will force the banks to lend" is particularly notable here), and lack of replacement capital, the only way banks could make new loans was to

break up current borrowers and "reclaim" as much of the funds that they could get away with.

Whatever the reasons banks behaved as they did, their actual behaviour is indisputable; in operating a post-2009 regime that was very disadvantageous to existing borrowers, especially those to whom they had sold swaps.

Bank staff alternatively took on the personae of mentors and bully boys, according to immediate income targets and progress of their strategic plans to recover loans from now inadequate borrowers; and the risk of angry clients disrupting their plans.

Clearly, it was important not to be so aggressive that proprietors 'walked away' - the plan was to create a climate of fear, then feed insolvency practitioners a steady stream of business, so that the recession could be credibly blamed.

Banks often imposed major changes at inconvenient times, (or when they found out that the proprietor was on holiday). This was designed to disorientate the client and dissuade them from disagreeing with any bank demands.

Support from major accountancy firms added a layer of credibility to the process. The recession proved a bean feast for these firms, acting as "business advisors", issuing overpriced reports, whose fees the banks then doubled, taking the extra for themselves.

Finally, those accountancy firms acted as insolvency practitioners, ignoring the effects of the swaps (which had often been cancelled once the business was irrecoverable), and breaking up those firms. Ironically, if a swap prevents a firm from refinancing, and that firm cannot pay off all of its loans in the short term, a bank can technically deem it insolvent, as it can always raise its charges until they become unsupportable. Banks acquired a reputation for the sharpest of practices, especially RBS and Lloyds, who had received substantial financial government support, and whose ability to raise funds from other sources was now quashed. Support firms and units such as the notorious Global Support Group ("GRG"), West Register, Cerberus and Isabel, gained an unwelcome public profile, in association with those banks. This has proven a major impairment to economic recovery, as potential borrowers wisely stay away from such operations, and hence the lack of demand for funding and rock bottom interest rates extending, now for over nine years.

The next chapter discusses the perceptions and responses of the SMEs who had been sold swaps, subsequent to the market crash at the end of 2008.

Victims were initially told "You're the only one to complain". This statement was shown to be manifestly untrue when SME victims began meeting, discussing their mutual experiences, and organising into groups. The first public meeting was held in October 2012, shortly after a House of Commons Backbench Debate on the subject.

These public meetings saw the emergence of those bank swap salesmen who had since set up as "advisors".

This has proven to be a very profitable practice, as there are many who still do not understand the risks involved in swaps.

EXAMPLE
CLIENTS PETER GRICE, PAUL CLARK, E3, AND RBS

I have put these three clients together, as each of them provided me with a different insight into how bank RBS operated, and operates. E3 has asked to remain anonymous in the light of ongoing legal action. Their cases have all appeared in national press and TV.

Peter Grice ran a medium sized, successful business linked to food retailing. The essence was storage under precise conditions, in order to stop the food from spoiling. I have called this Limited. Peter had built a personal property portfolio, which he managed in a separate company, I have called this Properties.

Peter had been in this business for well over 20 years, and in 1988 had set up his own firm with a £100 redundancy payment. Having met him a number of times, he came across as a quiet and thoughtful man – certainly one to be prudent in his business behaviour. This view was reinforced by a review of his business books, they are carefully produced and diligently kept up to date in a highly methodical manner.

RBS spent time and effort in persuading Peter to do business with them, and transfer his loan accounts from another bank to them and provided refinancing for both Limited and Properties. However, there was a sting in the tail. On 4th December 2006, a persistent and garrulous saleswoman, Sneha

Patel, changed Peter's life and that of his family and employees in a catastrophic way.

She pestered the company and its representatives in order to sell her swaps. She told Peter's accountant that "Peter had agreed the deal, and was anxious to proceed". Peter denies he ever said this.

What she first did was to close deals with Peter on two derivative contracts, a 5 year £3.25 million collar for the Operations business, and a 10 year £1.8 million collar for Properties. Additional fees were charged to top-up Sneha's profit on the deal, about £2,500 per quarter for Operations, and £1,500 per quarter for Properties. Although the fees were transparent, the hidden risks associates with each of these contracts were not.

The levels of quarterly fee disguised the risk for each contract. The swap sold to Operations made the bank a net day one profit of 1.6% of the loan value, and the Properties one 3.3%. Sneha and her team would have earned around 10% of this amount for the sale – around £110,000 of day one bank profit and £11,000 in sales commissions. Clearly, both amounts justify a substantial amount of work from Sneha and her colleagues.

To answer the question "why the difference?", the answer is likely to have been the properties. As swap sales generated substantial capital risk, the greater asset base of Properties was exploited. Remember, the percentage represented the amount the bank gained, in return for exposing the client to risk. Looking at *gross* downside, the Operations figure was 1.8% and that for Properties 4%.

To get a feel for these numbers, imagine you were trying to insure the properties against fire or flood, etc. 4% (or even 1.8%) would represent a sizable premium, and substantial risk. Properties was exposed to that risk in the derivatives market, and the bank received 4% of the value.

Accordingly, as the value of protection (as opposed to exposure) of these contracts was minor, one has to ask whether the description "hedging" was misleading.

There was worse to come. In March 2008, the Properties collar was replaced with a 10-year swap for £3.6 million, increasing to £4.8 million in six months. The saleswoman doubled the original notional, and added on an additional £1.2 million, which coincided with a marked low in the forward yield curve used for swap pricing. In other words, the product was designed to squeeze every last iota of profit out of the client that it could – and up-risk his personal position accordingly.

To show this, the following graph illustrates the expected cash flows on the day the contract was sold.

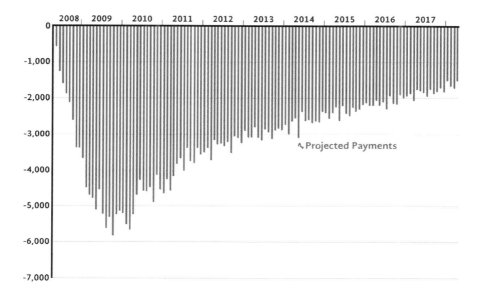

I look at this graph when I listen to the telephone conversation between the saleswoman and Peter, where she gives a repeated assurance, supported by much international 'evidence' that "interest rates are going to rise". She and her colleagues would, at the same time, have been looking at the above graph as she spoke, showing how much profit they expected to make from the market's pricing of rate falls.

Post 2008, the actual position got a lot worse, and this product was about £1 million in the hole by March 2009. It recovered to a negative £600,000 over the next six months, where it stayed for over a year, but, by then, it was too late. Peter's businesses had been forced into the bank's 'business support' unit. Insolvency Practitioners were involved, who appear to have taken the bank's version of everything as gospel.

One incident stands out among all of this wreckage. At one point, Peter had raised funds from another source, in order to try and buy back one of his properties, which the IP had put up for auction. A manager at RBS refused to include his bid in those considered, even though it was the highest bid. Whether this reflects the continued desire of RBS to control Peter's businesses, or was just done out of spite, is unknown. It does, however, reflect the mind-set of that bank's employees.

Peter is now struggling to purchase the rights to his former business. This needs, effectively, to be done third hand; is time consuming, costly, and difficult. Peter is continually chased by RBS, in respect of his other assets and they continue to try and make his life as difficult as possible.

Paul Clark had a successful haulage and storage business, and had acquired the business of handling the books of an internationally renowned children's author (no names – but think of wizards and glasses). Clearly, things looked particularly rosy for Paul, until he had the misfortune to be wooed by RBS.

Paul was involved with a derivative sale with another bank, prior to his involvement with RBS.

In March 2008, Sneha Patel sold Paul what she called a "Value Collar" in connection with a loan, again without describing the capital issues and risks involved. As with Sneha's sale to Peter Grice, the product was unnecessarily complicated, designed around profitability and disguising the downside via minimising early payments to the bank.

Post the 2009 crash, the value of this and associated risk, ballooned against him. When collateralisation is added to the position, the swap is a horrendous, downgrading force on the company's capital position.

In November 2010, the bank broke the swap, but by then the damage was done. By September, the company had already been pushed into Voluntary Administration.

Mid 2014, RBS finally made a redress offer in respect of the collar – again, by then it was too late. A creditors' meeting in 2013 put the company into liquidation.

Paul went through the same "Business Support" experience as Peter – the bank simply piled charges upon charges. These would have swallowed up any redress, especially as a replacement product was "justified" under the FSA/FCA review.

Clearly, all businesses went through the recession at this time, and would have undergone stress to their financial models. However, derivative sales would have had a substantially deleterious effect on business management, not only due to revenue, capital value, and collateralisation issues, but on the mindset of the business owner. He has been converted by the bank to being an amateur derivatives speculator, and it is hard to pilot a business through a recession with a snake sitting in the co-pilot's seat.

The general bank response to all of these arguments is "You would have gone bust anyway", and, as to the truth of this, well, nobody knows. However, banks are now regarded as untrustworthy in the business community, despite attempts from surprising sources to "big them up", and SME's are not open to being fooled for a second time.

Client E3 is memorable for three reasons – first, a part of his sale story, second, written advice given to him from an ex-salesman "expert", and thirdly, the experience of sitting through his 'independent review' in RBS's offices. Otherwise, his experience was similar to those of Peter and Paul.

Client E3 was a successful provider of alternative medical therapy, involving a number of sites, who sought finance from RBS. E3 was either a partnership, or a firm owned by individuals, depending on whose version you believe.

A derivative offer was being described, and a number of support staff were there. The talk was, surprise, surprise, of how interest rates were going to rise. E3 asked "what if interest rates fall?" Four voices immediately said, in chorus, "Interest rates are going to rise". Clearly, that was RBS's rehearsed mantra. We may set this scene to music!

E3 was sold swaps by RBS in November 2007 and July 2009. At the second date, the market had obviously crashed, and the bank would have known the initial swap was a serious hamper for the business.

E3's business went the way of the others – but then E3 went to an ex swaps salesman "advisor" to get help. I was astounded by what he showed me.

The "advice" is in the form of a 25-page letter, which is clearly intended to be sent to the bank as a letter under the clients' names. It starts in a professional manner, but becomes dangerously abusive by the bottom of page 3. It has clearly been produced by someone who believes derivative sales concealing certain risks (capital significance) are adequately described by the word "hedging", as long as break costs are described in the process.

While triple exclamation marks may be suitable to impress reviewers under the FCA regime (for whom the letter seems to have been directed), they would sit ill within a document intended for Court.

It is enlightening, however, in describing mis-selling sanctions as "what would be considered fair" - a totally meaningless comment, as, if the product is described as "hedging", and significant risks omitted, then *no* level of profit is "fair". However, neither the FSA or FCA publicly specified any limits on profitability; (both were remarkably coy about this, and still are), so that point is moot.

Less amusing was the visit to RBS's headquarters, where I accompanied the client E3, to meet two bank representatives (I have called WC and WD) and an 'independent reviewer' (known as an "IR"). After initial introductions, the IR described herself and her role – from a standard script. She was a junior solicitor, and clearly any knowledge about derivatives would have been both recent and shallow. When she had finished, I attempted to ask her a question – I was immediately rebuffed by WC, who insisted that the IR was not allowed to answer any questions. All of the talking was to be done by WC and WD.

How any professional person can allow themselves to be gagged like that is a mystery to me – it underlines the weakness of the FCA in allowing the banks to impose such a system.

It got worse. At one point E3 complained that the bank had been denigrating him behind his back – and, astoundingly, they had been naïve enough to put such insults *into writing*, which they then copied him into. When he complained about this, WD said "This interview is to be conducted in a respectful manner". *They then insisted on leaving for five minutes - "while we calmed down"*. Bearing in mind that RBS had perpetrated what was, to all intents and purposes, a "protected fraud" (the protection being the clauses in the documentation), this behaviour beggars belief. It reinforced in my mind the need for such processes to be carried out in court as banks appear to run any other process to their own advantage and by any means possible. I am grateful that I have never had to work with such grotesque people.

While I am on the subject – one advantage of court is that judges and barristers insist on evidence being questioned and gone through thoroughly – and they are experts in detecting lies and dissembling. I can also honestly say that, having met Peter, Paul and E3 more than once, I would trust them a lot. The bank staff had the mien of mobsters in suits.

5.
HOW THE SMES THEN SAW IT

"The worthy officer started from Putney police station to find you, and walked into the queerest trap ever set in this world. When the front door opened he walked straight on to the stage of a Christmas pantomime, where he could be kicked, clubbed, stunned and drugged by the dancing harlequin, amid roars of laughter from all the most respectable people in Putney. Oh, you will never do anything better. And now, by the way, you might give me back those diamonds."

G.K. Chesterton – The Innocence of Father Brown

When the first complaints arrived concerning interest rate swaps, a common retort from the banks was "You've been the only one to complain", and similar expressions of surprise. Clearly, banks were aware of a major scandal brewing, and were keen to defer and try and defuse any complaints, minimising bad publicity as far as possibly. It is important to remember that, what to most people working in banking seemed an ingenious but inexplicable source of extra wealth generated by "Harry Potter" like swaps salesmen and departments, was turning out to be a living nightmare. It is also important to remember that banks were in a weakened state, both in terms of their capital positions and their public reputations, (for their competence and ethics), and they could not tolerate any more bad news.

However, it was only a matter of time before individual victims started to speak, meet, and then take action. Probably the most well-known group, and possible the largest, is Bully Banks (which has since attempted to rebrand as Ordinary People in Business, but still retains its public presence under its former name). They first held meetings in the West Country on a kitchen table, and then between its future directors in Bicester. This group was founded in December 2011, nearly three years after the visible impact of the derivative sales was first felt in its full force, by those unfortunate enough to have been sold them.

Bully Banks was led by Jeremy Roe, a charismatic orator, who addressed groups of 200 and more disgruntled borrowers in public meetings. The first of them was in Birmingham in Autumn 2012, shortly after the first House of Commons debate on the subject, described by Guto Bebb, and covered in detail in Chapter 7. My main memories of that meeting were of Mr Fraser Whitehead of solicitors Slater and Gordon, presenting a very long mathematical formula in an attempt to promote the services of his firm (the formula was, in fact, the financial equivalent of "2 + 2 = 4", but not many people were to know that). Another diversion was provided when Mr Abhishek Sachdev, a former derivatives salesman from Lloyds Bank who had subsequently set up as an expert and stood up to defend the derivative sales. A stentorian voice from the back row retorted with the trenchant comment "Shouldn't have sold the ******* thing then". This, together with the comment from my accountant, (if a bank is trying to sell it to you, it must be @$%^£!...") turned out to be the truest words, that I believe, have been uttered in this whole sorry affair.

Important work was also done by Insolvency Assist, driven by Jon Welsby, who is another tireless, highly motivated and shrewd campaigner. He lost his business through a derivative mis-sale (although his bank would argue that the derivative was irrelevant). Jon focuses on companies that have become insolvent, and therefore have lost any power to litigate against banks, as any action needs to be driven by the Insolvency Administrators.

Long term fixed rate loans, branded as "Tailored Business Loans", also had a champion a Mr John Glare, (not to disregard the tireless work of Ms Fiona Sherriff of Bully Banks and Heather Buchanan, of the Fair Business Banking APPG); who set up a group to address the sales of such loans by Clydesdale and Yorkshire Banks, both owned and assisted by National Australia Bank.

His website, http://www.nabcustomersupportgroup.org contained a lot of useful information; including an article from Mr James Ducker, another ex-bank swap salesman turned expert. He derived a process of reorganising loan capital repayments in order to "fit" the derivative, which, while being ingenious, disregarded the commercial considerations that usually come with such loans. John is perhaps better known for appearing dressed in a deerstalker and armed with a megaphone, with two supporting ladies holding a large banner in front of Clydesdale Bank branches, while he broadly denounces the behaviour of the bank. John was "sold" a fixed rate loan by Clydesdale.

As a business borrower who was deemed fully responsible for contracts, he entered into on behalf of his company, he therefore lost his legal claim. What is interesting about this case is the fact that Clydesdale stated publicly that "they should have sold him a loan with a shorter duration". Why state this? This may reflect the covert "FSA test" for derivatives that was used in the FSA/FCA review (for a bank's accountant, derivatives and the fixed part of fixed rate loans are all the same anyway).

Newer entrants, and the rising stars of the action groups, are Nikki and Paul Turner, who have formed SME Alliance, which addresses a broader spectrum of bank misbehaviour. They have successfully "carried the banner" forwards, having personally fought a long (over nine years!) campaign against a bank which appears to have determined to stop at nothing in order to conceal the truth. At their most recent conference, some clients flew in from Ireland to explain how mis-selling worked there; (a story as grotesque and disheartening as that of the UK, but with its own unique features[5]).

I should also mention Steve Middleton, who has a background in both being an IFA and working in a senior position in a bank, so knows both sides of the coin. I have worked personally with Steve and his partner Jon Hill. Steve in particular seems to have a particularly strong grasp of bank regulation. I look forward to seeing him give evidence in the witness box.

The long term effects of swap mis-selling are likely to dwarf both those of pension mis-selling (1988 – 1994), and PPI mis-selling (2000 on). With the first, most victims had not yet reached pension age, and could be compensated via being reinstated into a former pension scheme (at a cost, payable by the vendor, of additional payments) - and PPI should, in the vast majority of cases, be solvable via a refund of premiums plus interest.

Pension mis-selling has all but been cleared up - however, banks are continuing to struggle to finalise PPI mis-selling redress. The main problem is not that cases are hard to handle once identified – it is the techniques used by the Claims Management Companies (CMCs), which use similar scatter-gun tactics to those used by banks when they sold the products. The CMC first garners a list of names and addresses from TV, press advertising or unsolicited phone calls – then presents this list to all the banks involved, demanding that they identify any loans that the client may have had with them. As the banks' systems, by all accounts, are somewhat old and creaking, the process is interminable, involving aircraft hanger sized open plan offices, full of staff taking calls and researching bank databases. One does occasionally feel some sympathy for these banks – however, their predicament is no-one's fault but their own. The old underworld adage "If you can't do the time, don't do the crime" seems apt here.

As a last word on the PPI process, a small debt of gratitude is due to Mr Antonio Horta-Osorio, the first banking executive who publicly recognised the problem, and chose to announce reserves to cover it in Lloyds Bank's books. However, this would not have got him much popularity in the banking world, and may have accounted for his problems with stress. In my view, this

---

[5] SME Alliance have had some notable recent success – see their website https://www.smealliance.org/.Nikki and Paul Turner managed to put five Lloyds Reading bankers in prison for 50 years.

recent unfortunate publicity over certain activities is overshadowed by his announcement on PPI – in my experience, he is the first senior executive in the world of banking who has proactively told the truth about wrongdoing. However, Lloyds still mis-sell swaps.

Swap mis-selling was different from the previous two mis-selling scandals. Whereas the other two could be regarded as reasonable products being sold to inappropriate people, swap mis-selling was carefully and cynically planned, with a cleverly calculated intention of profiteering by exposing clients to risk. The borrower was deliberately exposed to additional risk, which was covertly secured using the loan covenant information, to which the bank had access. This was far worse than other mis-selling scandals, which could be pictured simply as feeding frenzies where the game had gone too far.

When banks lend money, their loan covenants state, in brief, "If things go wrong, we'll take it back – or worse". Clearly, a bank has a right to take action if its expected repayments look in jeopardy. However, to secretly extend this "asset lasso" to include risks inherent in the swap sale, when so much key information had been concealed on the sale, is an iniquity that stands apart. Effectively, the covenant package now said – "We'll add other things that could make it go wrong. Then, if things go wrong, we'll blame you for everything, then take it back – or worse". Downside risk coverage was all assigned to the borrower.

The swaps delivered all of the risk and none of the finance of the original loans. When the market turned, the banks were left with inadequate security for their derivative sales (as there is no liquid market for SME loans, but the opposite very much holds true for derivatives). The revised picture rendered the banks overexposed to the businesses to which they had lent.

At this point, the use of GRG-type units, which, up until then, had primarily been used as recovery support units (although at a price – see Roger Lane-Smith's description in Chapter 4 of how those bank units worked), were corralled into fund raising units for those banks. Bearing in mind the public unpopularity of the original bailouts, no more public funds were likely to materialise. And yet the new PRA (Prudential Regulatory Authority) and Treasury (via the Asset Protection Agency) were demanding adequate bank solvency quickly (i.e. money in the balance sheet); and clearly did not pay too much attention as to where it had come from.

For an example of how this framework operated, see the "Buzzfeed Dash for Cash" revelations.[6]

Borrowers who were unable to refinance had little choice but to sign up the GRG units, thus losing much of their financial control. They were then subjected to whatever fee raising shenanigans the banks desired. One favourite method was to demand a "viability review", produced by a large accountancy firm. In exchange for a mass of information culled from management accounts and the proprietor themselves, the client was presented with a large invoice (always larger than that quoted), which was split between bank and reviewer. When the need for funds required it, or when the client became awkward, they could be "terminated" quickly. One way was for the bank to simply stop paying tax to HMRC – in which case the taxman was effectively used as a dupe to demand that the company be put into administration. With the help of obliging insolvency practitioners, who neither understood nor cared about derivative risk, (and the derivatives were often quietly sold off once the company was under bank control), the dirty work was concluded.

As the forward curve, which dictated derivative vales, dropped unpredictably from time to time the derivative debts would have increased, leading to harsher treatment from the banks. While this would have been inexplicable to the clients; the solvency savants at the banks would have known very well what was going on (not necessarily so the GRG teams, who would most likely have been kept in the dark). All that they would see was a command from "on high" to raise more funds. This has been confirmed by TV interviews of "moles", who worked within those units. They clearly thought that their leaders were making gratuitous demands for cash.

The banks' behaviour would have been unfathomable to the SMEs involved, who would have felt that they were dealing with the Mafia rather than respectable financial institutions. News of such behaviour would have spread through networking meetings – such as Chambers of Commerce, Federation of Small Businesses, and other networking groups. Further corroboration was provided by the press, Lawrence Tomlinson's report, and a smattering of

---

[6] https://www.buzzfeed.com/heidiblake/dash-for-cash?utm_term=.sywl2YQZ0#.ieyaWZlG7

lawsuits against the banks in question, primarily Barclays and RBS - particularly RBS.

The complete lack of trust in banks engendered by these practices has been demonstrated by SMEs' attitudes to borrowing since the end of 2008. Normally, the economy takes a few years to get back on its feet, and then borrowing picks up again, and things return to normal. Not this time. We have recently passed the seventh year of a record breaking low in UK (and world) interest rates. Bearing in mind that interest rates are raised to regulate excessive borrowing, one can only conclude that the market is dead. The Bank of England are, effectively, begging businesses to borrow and revitalise the UK economy –and those businesses are turning round and saying no.

Of the businesses that have survived, different means of finance have been sought. The peer to peer lenders have received an exponential growth in custom since the crash. However, they are still finding their feet in the underwriting arena; and they can be unreliable and slow, if propositions are unusual or the security provided is weaker.

Other mechanisms are sought by SMEs, of which I have anecdotal evidence. I understand at least two victims have set up internet operations offshore, with local funding, and where taxation may be paid locally, at a lower rate than in the UK. I have heard of schemes to secure assets and income outside the reach of lending banks, buy using methods that sounded dubious to me. These businessmen had always come across to me as honest, while being hard negotiators, and would have been ready to pay taxes on the usually accepted basis. Now, in the light of banks which gouged them, and regulators who stood by and let it happen, the taxman may have a harder job in replacing that income from the same people.

Doubtless, the UK economy will eventually return to full output, and "business as usual" – but it has crawled along the floor for seven years, and has actually worsened during that time (as evidenced by our friend, the forward curve again! - this is before the Brexit protest vote.)

The next chapter investigates the role and behaviour of the hapless Financial Services Authority, who regulated this field during the mis-selling period. The FSA was the regulator at the time that swap selling with loans became more prevalent, received a lot of criticism in the aftermath, and was disbanded in

2013. However, it does appear to have managed to apply some restraints on the worse aspects of swap mis-selling.

Political pressure on allowing banks to behave as they pleased made the regulators job difficult, if not impossible. However, some recent comments from those in charge at the time suggest that they still do not understand exactly what was going on.

EXAMPLE
CLIENTS F1 AND F2 – LLOYDS BANK

Client F1 ran a successful chain of holiday homes in the North of England. In conjunction with loan finance, bank V sold him both a 10 year £4m swap in June 2008, 4.5% for two years, rising to 5.48% after that. Lloyds granted itself a 3 year unilateral break option, which gives the bank more day 1 profit.

On the same date, Lloyds sold F1 a £4 million interest rate cap at 5.75% *in its own favour*. How this could have been 'sold' as hedging I cannot imagine. F1's business must be unique for having been sold "hedging" by Lloyds, and found that, in fact, *his company was actually hedging a bank in case of interest rate rises*". This takes the whole process of selling "hedging" towards farce, and shows the competence, or otherwise, of some of the salesmen and saleswomen. The only justification I can possibly find for such a sale is the apparent "2% for 10 years" FSA rule, designed to limit profit (and salesman's commission). The salesman probably got a good kicking from his manager for his idiocy – but would still have got his commission. (A good "kickback", too).

As it turned out, interest rates went the other way, and this contract caused minimal, if any, damage – it was the swap they sold that did the damage.

F1 was pushed into bankruptcy, and lost his business. His wife was shown on TV, having to personally provide cleaning services for apartments she and her husband once owned.

F2 was a structured collar offloaded by a celebrated character, working for Lloyds in the pomp of SME derivative sales, before becoming an "independent advisor". This is most memorable for the ignorance shown by the independent reviewers, who presented a "solution" to the original sale in the form of a replacement product, which was nearly as bad as the original. My colleague Gary Kendall had priced this up, identified the cynical attempt any the bank to avoid losing any of its ill-gotten profits, and gave them a mouthful. The bank staff visibly cringed at this, and Deloittes backtracked furiously – "of course, back at Head Office, we've got a whole team working on this".[7] This demonstrated the highly dubious nature of the review process – supervised by individuals who clearly had no idea of how to assess derivative risk.

One more snippet – at the meeting, the bank representative was accused of altering the bank's file record for his loan prior to an FSA/FCA inspection – and altering it back again afterwards. I have no idea as to whether this was true, but the rep's rate of sweat production, already high, seemed to increase to a flood after these words were spoken. I hope that he was paid well.

At a second meeting, a new product was presented – which was actually worse than the first offer made! We then realised both the attitude that banks were taking to this review, and the skill – or lack of it – provided by the "skilled persons" who oversaw it. However, by now, the bank representatives had learned their lines. The answer to virtually every question asked was "The FCA has said that this offer is Fair and Reasonable." This mantra must have been repeated at least ten times at the meeting. As an exercise in justifying any decision to a client, it was worse than useless.

I have only attended one other such review meeting under the FSA/FCA's review process – described in the previous chapter - and refuse to attend any more. They demonstrate the totally cynical attitude that banks have (and had, in the mis-selling era) towards anyone naïve enough to do business with them. My prognosis is grim – by destroying their honest clients, they will be left with the others – I have heard of banks being left with property assets as an aftermath to induced bankruptcy, then having to sell them on to dubious new clients (with the provision of extra bank finance), and showing every sign that their wonderful new client will clean up, load up, and disappear.

In other words, such banks will end up with only mugs and crooks as customers. The bank will gouge the mugs, and the crooks will gouge the bank. Not a healthy way for anyone to be in any business!

---

[7] The other Accountant /Management Consultant claim is "we're all working around the clock on this".

6.
HOW THE FSA SAW IT

"They would have boomed the miracle. Then they would have bust up the miracle. And what is the worst, they would have proved that I was in the conspiracy. It would have been our sham miracle. That's all there is to it; and about as near hell as you and I will ever be, I hope."

G.K. Chesterton — The Incredulity of Father Brown

The FSA was tasked with regulating sales of financial products to individuals, not companies; and, indeed, was only given any role in supervising residential mortgages relatively late in its existence. It never had any control over corporate lending, which was generally determined by contract; and, as corporate borrowers could avail themselves of advice from accountants and lawyers, was thought not to require consumer protection. If a commercial borrower did not take sufficient care in using such professionals to advise him of the effects of various types of borrowing, that was his lookout. However, neither of these professions proved capable of supporting their clients in the face of an extremely cunning and determined bank process to deliberately mislead.

The Financial Services Authority, set up by Gordon Brown in 2001, was given direct responsibility for regulating banks and other financial institutions; – not only their solvency and stability, but also their sales and marketing techniques. It replaced the Securities and Investments Board (SIB); the Personal Investment Authority (PIA), former regulator of life assurance and personal pension products; Investment Management Regulatory Organisation (IMRO); and, more importantly, the Bank of England in respect of their role of supervising the banks. It can be regarded as the first "Omni-Regulator" of modern times, and its duties were truly awesome.

Its board was appointed by the Treasury, although it operated independently of government. However, in reality, this gave the Treasury much direct control over this regulation, as individuals could be appointed or removed at political whim. Accordingly, a system of nods and winks was likely to emerge, with politicians publicly appearing to stand away from the key decisions (and therefore avoiding any blame if things went wrong); while leaving regulators to "read the signs", possibly provided by "special advisors". (Such methods were common under the Blair government, which perceived the dangers of the (mostly) openly interventionist tactics under the Thatcher administration). Whereas previously systems of self-regulation separate for, e.g., banks and insurance companies, had been the norm; the new system - an "omni-regulator" with one person responsible - was prone to unattributable interference.

A good example of this was Tony Blair's "red tape" letter sent to Callum McCarthy, the head of the FSA in July 2005, where he makes a general attack on "red tape" (a straw man which anyone can criticise), which was described in the Sun.[8]

Reading between the lines, this is directed towards restrictions on bank lending- that lending generates short-term popularity and the illusion of personal wealth, but generates all too familiar risk. Two years later, Northern Rock got into well-publicised trouble from over-lending, and indulging in the illusion that collateralisation could address market risk. (They were not the first organisation to fall to this illusion).

Six years later, in December 2011, the FSA generated the wonderfully alliterative headline "FSA blames Blair, Brown and Balls for RBS collapse."[9]

The "Light Tough, Limited Touch" approach was criticized heavily in the article, to which Labour responded by criticism of David Cameron and George Osborne.

In 1997, the setting of base rate was separated from (Brown's own) political control, and a new independent committee, the Bank of England Monetary Policy Committee (MEPC) was set up.

While the control of short term interest rates was always part of the UK government's monetarist policy for stimulating or dampening the economy, it might be subject to political interference in a way that was not in the long term interests of the UK. For example, the UK economy "overheating" might require rate rises to dampen it, but an imminent election might make such rises unpopular. By divesting himself of this power, Mr Brown removed any opportunity for the government to fudge the issue.

However, Mr Brown also believed that long term fixed interest rate (LTFR) mortgages would remove volatility from the housing market. This belief, shared by, among others, Alistair Darling and Grant Schapps, was supported by Professor David Miles' report produced in 2004. An FT article of July 2007 described this belief.[10]

---

[8] http://www.thesun.co.uk/sol/homepage/news/3104178/Tony-Blairs-bank-bombshell-He-wanted-LESS-regulation.html

[9] http://www.standard.co.uk/news/fsa-blames-blair-brown-and-balls-for-rbs-collapse-6377806.html

[10] http://www.ft.com/cms/s/0/74de20f4-3011-11dc-a68f-0000779fd2ac.html#ixzz3rSynQQN8

This report is remarkable for suggesting, in its Appendix A, a template for advising *residential borrowers* on LTFR mortgages. The report included part of the forward curve of 12 February 2004. (I have replicated the figures from Bank of England data.) What the report does not include, is the fact that the Bank of England produces figures, not for eight years, *but for twenty-five*. The information omitted tells a somewhat different story...

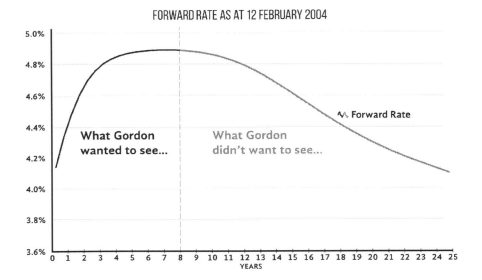

FORWARD RATE AS AT 12 FEBRUARY 2004

Nothing to the right of the black dashed line was shown in the report.

The second issue is the wording in the report, describing what this curve is:

> Predicting the future of interest rates is no science. However, a useful pointer to what the cost of borrowing might be over the next five years can be found in how the financial markets view the future. The following chart reflects how those who trade in financial markets see how interest rates might move in the future. The figures are taken from Bank of England estimates www.bankofengland.co.uk/statistics/yieldcurve.

This curve does NOT simply describe how those who trade in financial markets see how rates might move in the future. It indicates the rates at which trades are made on that day, in respect of future positions. The distinction is vital, as Miles' description ignores any effects driven by the term structure of interest rates – an issue well understood by all actuaries. Interestingly, of over 100 organisations included as having been consulted in Appendix C, the Actuarial Profession is not included; although some actuarial firms Hewitt Bacon & Woodrow and Tillinghast Towers Perrin are on the list.

This misinterpretation – which we could call "Gordon's Gaffe" (or, less kindly, "Brown's Balls-Up") gives a green light to swaps mis-selling.

I believe that four important questions need to be asked here:

– The first is – if you had been a borrower in 2004 – and taken Messrs Miles and Brown's "advice" in locking into a long-term fixed rate – how would you have felt in March 2009, just five years into the "Miles Curve", when base rate fell to 1/2% per annum? Moreover, as rates have stayed at under 1% per annum for nine years now, you would now feel you had paid dearly for your trust.

Luckily, the report falls shy of recommending 25-year fixes outright – but it would be interesting to see how many borrowers would have taken the inference that "the longer the fix, the safer".

Of course, in 2004 no-one could have predicted the timing, extent or duration of the fall – but the fact remains that such a contract exposes a borrower to these risks. That is why - even with interest rates at 1/2% - so few people opt for LTFR mortgages.

– The second point is – did the banks see this report as a "heads up" from the government that it would be OK to sell swaps to SME's? When the start of Pension mis-selling is compared with this process, (pension mis-selling started with Margaret Thatcher's "Man in the Sack" advertising, encouraging a few large insurers into a selling frenzy) and compared with the message given from this report – I believe that the answer must be "yes".

– The third point is – if you were a mortgage sales regulator under such government behaviour – what do you do? Public advice as to the risks of long-term fixed rates would *not* have met with the Government's approval – to say the least! The wrath of Gordon Brown – and the Treasury!

– And fourth – a falling yield curve show lack of confidence in the economy – not something that any government wants to broadcast!

One can almost hear the discussions between banks and the regulator – "If Gordon Brown wants us to promote LTFR mortgages to *individuals*, how can you complain when we sell derivatives which do the same thing to *businesses*? Businesses are not covered by COBS (the FSA's Conduct of Business rules), and therefore what we sell to them is nothing to do with you. Tony Blair has publicly criticised excessive red tape in bank regulation (June 2005) – we are selling innovative products which meet the government's aims. End of argument. Go away."

What it appears that the FSA actually did was, under the circumstances, properly understood, quite resourceful, and they probably regulated effectively as far as they could under the circumstances. The process was the same as that which was used for life assurance and pensions salesmen – to restrict the commission payable on each sale. This was achieved by using the fact that bank commissions were usually related to bank profit; so restricting profit had the same effect as restricting commissions.

I was first made aware of this when I read the following extract from a report prepared by one ex-salesman in August 2013; he had subsequently set himself up as a derivative and mis-selling expert:

"4.4. There is no clear definition about what is fair and reasonable profit or (sic) these OTC[11] derivatives. However, from our extensive experience in the Financial Markets across multiple banks, a sensible benchmark that is considered to be a fair and competitive level of profit (at the time in 2006 – 2008) is 20 basis points (*per year of term*) on an equivalent interest rate swap. This is the methodology I have applied in this report. This is within the bounds *of what some banks had agreed with the FSA in 2004/2005 when they first started to provide these derivatives to SMEs.*" (my italics).

Such a test has been confirmed to me by one other ex-salesman advisor, and another expert who did not personally sell swaps to SMEs.

---

[11] OTC means 'Over the Counter, i.e., not traded on a recognized exchange.

The rest of our expert's report discusses what the writer and his colleagues consider to be a "fair" commission, as judged by the writer and his colleagues. It also gives some valuable definitions of "CEE", the bank's measure of risk in excess of the current market value of the derivative.

The problems with this approach are as follows:

1) A successful sale (as carried out between 2006 and 2009) involves both generating a bank profit, and avoiding positive cash flows (to the bank) in the early period of the contract, which would give the game away. How easy or difficult this is depends on the disposition of the forward curve, on the date of the sale. The shape of this curve was, is, and always will be, difficult to predict accurately.

2) Banks had invested substantial resources in their SME derivative sales forces – recruitment, training, compliance, other supervision, motivation, and weeding out non-performers were and are expensive. It was therefore imperative to "keep the expensive sales force selling", no matter what the shape of the curve.

3) To avoid early positive cash flows, it would have always been necessary to construct products around the curve. Sometimes this was easy (e.g., in Autumn/Winter 2007, the curve dropped like a stone – a straightforward swap would have met the criteria). However, if the early period of the curve demonstrated a rise (as with the Miles Curve), it would be more difficult: – the "hump" in the curve makes it hard for the pricer (the derivatives trader) to achieve *both* profitability *and* avoid early positive flows. At these times, neither straightforward swaps, nor collars would fit the bill. The solution to this was to design products where the downside (floor) was "geared up" to achieve a greater rate of profit from the floors. Once this was done, the initial level of the floor could be lowered in order to avoid the early positive flows, and sales could be closed without the purchaser realising he had locked himself into a time bomb.

4) The element of long term risk in any swap product as measured by the

vast derivative swaps market, can therefore vary substantially, depending on when it was sold.

5) Looking at it another way, using the net bank profit (and commission) as a measure depends on the difference between client benefit and client detriment. A more acceptable product might involve less aggressive levels of both, (e.g., a 'wide jawed collar', with high cap and a low floor). However, this would generate less profit per sale. By using artificial "long term boosters" on the floor, the profit could be initially jacked up, then metered down by lowering the level of the cap. Accordingly, a "high reward high exposure" product would pass the 20 basis point test, as well as our wide collar would.

6) The "swaps game" was actually seen by those in the know at the banks as dubious, and therefore the process was run as a fire sale, with high pressure on the salesmen, and challenging production targets. This was because the falling forward curve presaged a slump. Once interest rates actually did fall, it would have become impossible to produce products which were both profitable and avoided early positive cash flows. Of course, a fall so rapid, deep and chronic was not forecast.

7) In chapters 4 and 5, I have covered in more detail the banks' philosophies and practices, according to the epithet "If things go wrong, we'll take it back' – or worse". The banks' careful assessment of the "CEE" cover indicated their intentions to expand the list of "things to go wrong"; – which, clearly, were not divulged to their clients.

8) Banks held themselves out, and were trusted to, provide loan underwriting services to both themselves and their clients. Although the loan underwriting process gave no legal duties towards the borrower on this behalf, there was a clear expectation from borrowers that, if the bank was actually prepared to lend money, they had made a dispassionate and principled decision as to the creditworthiness of the borrower.

With the advent of interest rate swap sales, all of that changed. Banks were now seen as capable of selling destructive products along with loans, which reduced the creditworthiness of the borrower. Banks thus branded themselves as untrustworthy in the eyes of SME borrowers. Who would be foolhardy enough to borrow from such people, when the loan (and swap) could be used to dole out the "GRG treatment" if the bank needed to (and possibly, just if the bank wanted to?). Any concept of a bank being "fair and reasonable" went straight out of the window.

Although most SMEs still do not actually understand what banks did wrong, they no longer trust them. The death of conventional borrowing, evidenced by the 1/2 % -odd base rate for nine years – shows that distrust in a way that no volume of argument could.

There were two more points that need to be made when considering the banks' behaviour. The first is that banks were providing substantial tax revenues to the government – and, in trying to support a socialist administration with no rises in income tax, this revenue was vital to them. Ministers would have been strongly dis-incentivised to take any steps to restrict this revenue.

The second is that most of the risks involved in swap mis-selling were described within the report and accounts of the banks in question. In fact, the wonderfully clear descriptions of those risks in those accounts could be used as a part of a training program for those who wanted to understand those risks. The only problem is that the definitions of various risks are sometimes different for different banks. So I use the definitions – i) cash flow risk (can't pay your bills), ii) market risk (negative equity), iii) credit risk (covenants at risk), iv) operational risk (everything else – as described earlier).

Banks had described those risks as "risks" in their own report and accounts – and then wrapped them up and sold them on as "hedging" to their borrowing clients.

It is also worth noting the Treasury Select Committee's comments in October 2012 regarding the FSA's statement post the RBS bail-out:

'In December 2010 the FSA initially felt that a 298-word statement about RBS's failure was explanation enough. This reflected serious flaws in the culture and governance of the regulator. It also reflected a fundamental misunderstanding of its duty to account for its actions to the public and Parliament.

'In view of the vast amounts of public money committed to propping up RBS, Lord Turner's comment that a Report into the demise of RBS "would add little, if anything, to our understanding of what went wrong" was inadequate. He should have grasped the need for a public explanation of how that situation had arisen; something which he has subsequently acknowledged. We would not expect the new chairmen of the regulators to repeat the error.'

George Osborne had announced his decision to replace the FSA in June 2010.

A final word. The man regarded as the first ever real management consultant, Mr Peter Drucker, wrote a ground breaking book, "The Effective Executive", first published in 1967. In this book, he describes "the impossible job" – which has responsibilities so large and/or diverse that the responsibilities of the job are impossible to achieve. In fact, it can strongly be argued (and appears to have been born out) that regulating more than one industry is too much for any one man. Professor Drucker cites the example of Robert McNamara the USA Secretary of State for Defence. (While Mac was a truly phenomenal human being, the same cannot be said for any of the senior officeholders of the FSA). I believe that combining supervision of banking with *any* other duties immediately creates the impossible job. It is noteworthy that the FSA ultimately regulated *every* sector of financial services, apart from company pension schemes. So that however talented and experienced the FSA senior staff, however dedicated and diligent their staff – the FSA would eventually be caught out. Clearly, the division of the FSA into FCA and PRA has done nothing to address the "omni-regulator" factor; where banks are lumped in with other financial organisations, and regulation continues to work on the "one size fits all" principle. I look at this further in chapter 9.

So, to summarise, the FSA's behaviour up until the end of 2008 can safely be said to be government led – the promotion of LTFR mortgages by the use of the forward curve (a practice still endorsed by the FCA, despite the fact that it is misleading) – in fact, not only endorsed, but compulsory! – focus on headline-grabbing minor infractions, while leaving major problems unaddressed – and over focus on insurers and IFAs, while leaving banks relatively untouched. It was no surprise that untrammelled lending practices, deliberate deceit concerning risk, and other base practices caught out, not only the UK's, but the whole world's banking industry.

The next chapter describes the contributions to the search for honest solutions by individual MPs. These MPs, working within All Party Parliamentary Groups, or groups, or singly, made enormous contributions to the emergence of the truth. They could hear their individual constituents' complaints, and understand the financial devastation that the mis-selling had created, both for companies, and their employees who had lost their jobs or been otherwise impoverished by bank behaviour.

Certain individual MPs must take enormous credit for their tireless work in exposing this scandal, amid their other heavy workloads.

EXAMPLE
THE CASE OF THE HUNDRED YEAR CLIENT
PAUL ADCOCK - ADCOCK AND SONS- BARCLAYS BANK

This case is also in the public domain, so protagonists may be named. It is also notable for three things:

1) The accurate description of the derivative sold in the press, an excellent piece of journalism by Robert Peston, allowing us all the information needed to price the contract without having ever seen the paperwork.
2) The first public exposure, I believe, of such a contract to the UK public.
3) Terminology.

1. THE DERIVATIVE

Paul Adcock's business, Adcock and Sons, was sold a "Structured Collar" by a Barclays Bank swap salesman, in connection with floating rate loan finance he took out, in early 2007.

What had actually happened is that Mr Adcock was inveigled into taking out a contract with Barcap, Barclays global investment bank, which ratcheted up his payments to 9% per annum, and this, ultimately just about trebled his costs.

Mr Peston describes the interest rate rules which the new contract imposed on Adcocks. But he misses the point when he states that "Back in 2007, it may well have been the consensus view of economists that interest rates were more likely to rise than fall". The bank (or, at least, the salesmen and their bosses) did not give a stuff about where interest rates were likely to go! They were using a mechanism called the forward curve – used by market traders and regulators alike – to value derivatives. The complicated bit is that when the layman talks about "interest rates" at any one date, a banker sees a *whole string* of dealing rates, each one relating to a different point into the future.

Using this curve allowed Barclays to do two things with the sale:

a) Design a product to sell to Adcocks that made the bank an immediate profit, and
b) Design a product where the damage due to risk exposure, was not immediately apparent to a layman.

The second reason is why structured collars were "invented "- NOT, as described by Martin Wheatley of the FCA, who stated, it was to sell products that were "too complicated for people to understand" – but to prevent the risk exposure from becoming immediately apparent from the early payments. The common claim by the mis-sold against banks was that "the bank knew interest rates would go down". None of them did. The philosophy was simply "If things go wrong, we'll take it (the loan) back – or worse". The bank took a day one profit. The borrower took the main risks.

A study of the forward curve around the beginning of 2007 indicates that a structured collar is necessary to achieve both a) and b) above.

2. THE PUBLIC EXPOSURE

The sale, and its aftermath, are explained masterfully in Robert Peston's book "How do we fix this mess?" It is difficult to improve on his detailed description, which I recommend reading in full.

His article in connection with BBC News in April 2012 cites small business owner Paul Adcock describing the derivative as "having torn the heart out of the business".

Adcocks had banked with Barclays since 1912 – virtually 100 years. The "new attitude to clients" adopted by banks was described, followed by this quotation from an unidentified "head of one bank" - "This doesn't feel as big as PPI. But let's be clear, we all went slightly bonkers a few years ago selling products that our clients didn't really need. We forgot to put the interests of our customers first." This was the understatement of the century.

These were NOT just "products that clients didn't really need." This was not just "forgetting to put the interests of our customers first". These products and the sales process were *designed* to make profits by *deliberately putting their clients in harm's way.*

3. TERMINOLOGY

For the third point, the term 'structured collar' has no recognised position amongst finance professionals. "Structured Finance" refers to the use of derivatives, while the terms cap, floor, collar and swap are the building blocks of this finance, and are used consistently by traders and other specialists. Other contracts are generally termed "exotics", and samples are generally found in derivatives textbooks. See, for example, the work of Professor John Hull. Other terms to be applied to options are "European" (= may be exercised at one point in time), "American" (= may be exercised at any time during a period[12]), and "Bermudan", (= may be exercised at a number of points during a period).

It does sound a bit like a detective story (Sherlock Holmes and the Case of the Structured Collar?) and, in fact, it is rather like one. Anyone who has read "The Speckled Band" knows the story involves a number of seemingly

---

[12] An interesting question can be asked here – if you own the American option rights on a swap – (you can take out a 5-year swap at a predetermined fixed rate any time in the next 3 years, say); if the value of the underlying swap is positive (i.e., you gain on exercising the option), should you then exercise the option? The answer, surprisingly, is no! You should first check the market price of the swap *with* the option – it is likely to be higher than that of the swap alone. Your financial position is likely to be better if you sell your deal, rather than if you exercise, and *then* sell.

innocent but ultimately sinister steps to 'create' a murder – the bed bolted to the floor, the air vent leading to the next room, the false bell rope – need only the addition of a swamp adder to create the desired effect. The Structured Collar was the answer to a bank's cost problem:

- the unpredictably malign behaviour of the "snake" (the forward pricing curve) compared with current base rate;
- the need for an expensive salesman to keep selling;
- the need for products to be superficially attractive in order to persuade the buyer;
- the need for a range of products, best if it's three – (excluding that pesky cap), to indicate a range of products from which the victim can *choose...* (like a Study in Scarlet, but where *all* the pills are poisoned...);
- so it can be made out that the purchaser was the author of his own misfortunes.

The best time to sell derivatives was when the forward curve fell consistently over time (i.e., sloped downwards). Then you could offer a swap at a rate lower than the current base rate, and still make money. The problem was when the curve rose, then fell (i.e., rose to a peak, then turned down). This could mean that your swap rate was higher than the current base rate. This means the product costs the punter money on day one. So it's harder to sell a swap.

The structured collar solves this. In essence, you sell a cap, but plus *two* floors instead of one. This doubles the profit based if rate falls, which you can take on day one. This helps you bring the cap level down.

7.
HOW THE MPS SAW IT

"If the devil tells you something is too fearful to look at, look at it. If he says something is too terrible to hear, hear it. If you think some truth unbearable, bear it."

G.K. Chesterton, The Wisdom of Father Brown

The issue of "Interest Rate Swap Mis-selling" has attracted much support from backbench MPs. This is partly due to the substantial numbers of individuals who claim to have been miss-sold. But it would be a mistake to assume that MPs only get involved in an issue where there are enough potential personal votes in it to justify it. MPs and their teams spend substantial amounts of time dealing with individual complaints, - just read "How to be an MP" by Paul Flynn, or "How to be a Parliamentary Researcher" by Robert Dale (both from Biteback Publishing). These books show the extraordinary lengths to which MPs go to help constituents – some correspondence trails can be up to 50 or 60 letters!

The MP who has done most to lead this cause has been Mr Guto Bebb, MP for Aberconway. He was originally alerted to the issues of interest rate swaps, and their financial cousins, fixed rate loans, by his constituents and a nearby contact from his college days, Mr Mansell Beechey;[13] the landlord of the Hen Lluw Du pub (Old Black Lion in English), who was persuaded to take out a fixed rate loan by Clydesdale Bank. The same bank is a former home of the celebrated financial genius Mr Fredrick Goodwin, who is mentioned elsewhere in this chronology. Mr Beechey's bank manager, whom he had known for many years, over lent and bumped him into a fixed rate loan, both of which would have increased the manager's sales commission.

Mr Bebb can be fairly described as the public face of Mis-selling Resistance, having provided major support, including the Chairmanship, for the All-Party Parliamentary Group for Fair Business Banking. He has instigated several backbench debates in the House of Commons on the subject, at which many MPs have raised issues regarding the poor experiences of their own constituents. I will pick up major points from these debates later in this chapter.

It is probable, that without Guto Bebb's intervention, the FCA review of mis-selling would have been even more delayed and weaker than it has actually turned out to be. While the review has proven a major disappointment to many participants, with its concealed reasoning and appointment of "independent skilled persons", many of whom are effectively bank stooges, it has provided satisfaction to some participants.

---

[13]Mr Beechey is a constituent of MP Mr Mark Williams, who has done much work on fixed rate loans.

Mr Bebb has now been promoted to Parliamentary Under-Secretary of State for Wales and has passed the baton for chairing the APPG, now re-named Fair Business Banking, to Calum Kerr MP and George Kerevan MP. There are currently over 100 all party MPs supporting this APPG.

Second, the Treasury Select Committee, under the Chairmanship of Mr Andrew Tyrie, have summoned several individuals from the banking industry to question them on their personal and their bank's behaviour. This has resulted in bringing some new information into the public domain, and some high-profile resignations, including those of Mr Chris Sullivan and Mr Derek Sach of RBS, who were publicly accused of misleading the Committee.

A close examination of the answers provided by some of the participants gives, to put it mildly, a significant degree of controversy as to the quality of the replies. Certainly, if they were expected to tell "the truth, the whole truth, and nothing but the truth", the central part of the answer was very much missing.

Clearly, bank executives cannot be expected to understand every detail of every aspect of how their organisations operate – but, for example, when the truth consists of "we sold product B rather than product A, because product B has extra hidden profit" – I find it difficult to believe that they are being open and truthful, if they don't, at least, *mention* the profit. Doubtless, a second visit to the Treasury Select Committee to answer these points will help them to put my mind at rest.

Also worthy of mention on the Treasury Select Committee are MPs Mark Garnier, and Lord Thurso. I have met Mark Garnier at an event in North Wales, to which he travelled well outside his constituency to meet mis-selling victims. I met Lord Thurso in similar circumstances at an Aberdeen meeting, attended by a large group of Tailored Business Loan victims. They have both invested significant time and energy into finding out the truth.

The production and presentation of the report "Changing Banking for Good" (June 2013), by the Parliamentary Commission on Banking Standards, chaired by Andrew Tyrie, clearly involved substantial work in its preparation, and contained much of interest. It cites interest rate swap mis-selling as a major blight on commercial lending to SME's, which it is worth quoting again here in full:

6) The interest rate swap scandal has cost small businesses dear. Many had no concept of the instrument they were being pressured to buy. This applies to embedded swaps as much as standalone products. The response by the FSA and FCA has been inadequate. If, as they claim, the regulators do not have the power to deal with these abuses, then it is for the Government and Parliament to ensure that the regulators have the powers they need to enable restitution to be made for this egregious mis-selling. (Paragraph 19)

All meaningful progress has effectively been blocked by HM Treasury, who pushed swaps into PFI deals.[14]

There have been four backbench debates, each led by Guto Bebb, as per the following table:

DATE	TOPIC	NUMBER OF SPEAKERS
21 June 2012	That this House has considered the matter of the mis-selling of interest rate swap products to small and medium-sized businesses; notes the work undertaken by the Financial Services Authority in this respect; and calls for a prompt resolution of the matter.	41
24 October 2013	That this House considers the lack of progress made by banks and the Financial Conduct Authority on the redress scheme adopted as a result of the mis-selling of complex interest rate derivatives to small and medium businesses to be unacceptable; and notes that this lack of progress is costly and has caused further undue distress to the businesses involved	51
4 December 2014	That this House has considered the Financial Conduct Authority's redress scheme, adopted as a result of the	32

[14] (see https://assets.publishing.service.gov.uk/government/uploads/system/uploads/attachment_data/file/225362/01_pfi_hedging120506.pdf)

	mis-selling of complex interest rate derivatives to small and medium sized businesses, and has found the scheme's implementation to be lacking in consistency and basic fairness; considers such failures to be unacceptable; is concerned about lack of transparency of arrangements between the regulator and the banks; is concerned about the longer than expected time scale for implementation; calls for a prompt resolution of these matters; and asks for the Government to consider appointing an independent inquiry to explore both these failings and to expedite compensation for victims.	
1 February 2016	That this House believes that the Financial Conduct Authority in its current form is not fit for purpose; and has no confidence in its existing structure and procedures.	29

The last topic, introduced some 3 ½ years after the first, is damning, although in that case the debate also covered the Connaught Fund collapse (not to be confused with the Connaught Plc collapse in September 2010 – in which interest rate swaps played an interesting, although concealed, role), as well as swap mis-selling.

The FCA was set up on 1 April 2013, after its predecessor was dissolved in disgrace. (The same staff covered mis-selling, however, as Mr Bebb discovered in his direct meetings with the regulator). They were then decapitated in July 2015, when George Osborne indicated in July 2015 that the appointment of their chief Executive, Mr Martin Wheatley, would not be renewed.

Mr Wheatley had become subject to criticism (in addition to the above) for an injudicious public statement in March 2014, concerning life insurance companies, which caused a depression in the market. In January 2015, both he and the FCA Chairman, Mr John Griffith-Jones, faced an uncomfortable 'grilling' from Andrew Tyrie and the Treasury Select Committee.

There is more information on the regulators in chapters 6 and 9. The information disclosed by the backbench MPs puts information into the public domain, that provides a fascinating insight into the mis-selling "programme", which has not, up to now, been revealed. Some of the more interesting contributions have been as follows *(my comments in italics)*:

Mr Guto Bebb: "The issue came to my attention in dealing as an MP with the hassles raised in constituency surgeries. It is a great advert for doing surgeries: we never know what will come through the door. Back in the autumn of last year, a constituent came in to talk about interest rate swaps, collars, caps and similar things. I was a self-employed business person for 15 years before I was elected to this place, and it crossed my mind that this businessman, who was talking about the loss of his business and his hotel and the potential loss of his house; might be finding an excuse for his business failure. I am not a hard-hearted individual, but I have been in business for a long time and I have the view that there is the rule of "buyer beware" in transactions with banks and other financial institutions. I therefore listened to his case attentively but with a degree of scepticism, wondering whether he was looking for an excuse for what happened to him.

The more I listened, however, the more I thought that there was something that I should look into, and the crux for me came when I tried to get hold of the verbal agreement between my constituent, Mr Colin Jones, and his bank. It took us a long time to get the bank to allow us to see a transcript of the verbal agreement, and by that point I understood something about the nature of interest swap derivatives and what was meant by swaps, caps and collars. I had a degree of understanding that we were not considering a straightforward financial product."

(Why would an honest bank withhold a transcript from an MP for so long?)

Damian Collins (Folkestone and Hythe) (Con): "I, too, congratulate my Hon. Friend on securing this debate. Does he share my concern about the experience of Castlewood Hotels in my constituency? It was sold such a product by the bank and told that if it did not accept it, its business could be in jeopardy in future."

(In fact, the bank knew that the opposite was true)

Emma Reynolds (Wolverhampton North East) (Lab): "I, too, would like to applaud the hon. Member for Aberconwy (Guto Bebb) for delivering such a fantastic speech. I want to tell the House about a similar case in my constituency. It is the case of Guardian Care Homes, and it has already been mentioned by my right hon. Friend the Member for Wentworth and Dearne (John Healey). The company's headquarters are in my constituency, but it employs about 900 staff in 30 care homes across the country. Small and medium-sized enterprises such as these need to be supported, rather than exploited.

I recently met members of the senior management at Guardian Care Homes, and I was shocked by what they told me. In 2007, they were sold two interest rate swap products, which were taken out against existing loans that had been taken out to improve the business model and to improve the care homes. They also said that the bank that sold them the products, told them that this was a condition of getting the original loans, and that the products would protect them against interest rate rises. They were not informed of the dangers and financial implications of interest rate falls, however. According to Guardian Care Homes, the bank did not at any point during the sale of those swaps fulfill its obligation to explain that such costs could be incurred.

Guardian Care Homes also discovered that the swaps that had been sold to them vastly exceeded the original terms of the loans, by 10 and 15 years respectively, which made things incredibly difficult for the company in the long term. An independent study of this specific case recently described the bank's behavior as reckless, and a complaint has been made against the bank. It beggars belief that banks were requiring SMEs to take these products alongside loans, and I look forward to hearing the Minister's response to these points today."

(Guardian Care Homes finally settled with Barclays after the High Court allowed him permission to call such witnesses as Bob Diamond, Jerry di Messier and Rich Ricci.)

Outside of the House of Commons, and some "after the event" input from the FSA and FCA, other formal consideration is minimal. It might be expected that the newly-established Banking Standards Board might have shown some interest in swap mis-selling, but anyone expecting this would be disappointed.

In their 2015/2016 annual review, interest rate hedging product mis-selling is mentioned once in the introduction, and that's it. Their Chairman, Dame Collette Bowe, gave a talk entitled "Better Bankers, Better Banks; "Strengthening Professionalism and Restoring Trust"[15] – which, while citing bad behaviour in general, then specifies the usual mantra "people taking risks that they didn't understand" – when the actual problem was that the middle people knew the risks very well – just dumped them on their clients; it was the ones at the top that were clueless.

She then speaks of professionalism, citing the medical profession, and the law. To put swap mis-selling into a medical context is like setting up a "Harold Shipman School of Palliative Medicine". However, she describes reputational risk well – "word gets round – you will destroy your business – you will be found out". To the degree that banks have abused the term loan market with swap mis-descriptions, nemesis is exemplified by the death of demand – a ½% or ¼% interest rate tells us that the borrowers just don't want to know. Dame Collette's following topic – "Trust" – describes what banks – and the economy – have lost.

The useful 49-minute recording comes alive in the 27th minute, with a contribution from the floor from Charles Jackson, a compliance and risk professional, who describes how things work in the real world, and how "whistle-blowers" get victimised, while the senior staff get off. Examination of the fortunes of whistle-blowers Nicholas Wilson (HSBC) and Paul Moore (HBOS) tell the same story. His view is that people need to walk the walk, not just talk the talk. Dame Collette's response included the words - "this (change in banking culture) is going to take a generation".

New City Agenda, a think tank established to challenge current thinking in financial services, may in future address the details of mis-selling.

The next chapter describes the role of the swap salesmen, without which there would have been no mis-selling. Ex bank swap salesmen have set themselves up as public advisors, with varying degrees of success. Whether the concealment of the same risks as before is part of the sales process, we do not know.

---

[15] http://www.bankingstandardsboard.org.uk/dame-colette-on-banking-standards-and-building-consumer-trust-in-the-banking-sector/

A single document, describing all of the hidden risks, would almost certainly prevent most mis-sales, but is unlikely to ever see the light of day, as the salesmen/advisors lack the integrity to use it.

Other ex-salesmen have obtained work under the regulator's swaps review, which, again, conceals the real risks. (Late note – now, apparently, back to (mis) selling with banks, targeting, inter alia, doctors' surgeries).

EXAMPLE
CRESTSIGN – A SEMINAL CASE

The next real-life case I have cited is that of Crestsign. This was a small company, owned by a director of Bully Banks, which settled with non-disclosure agreements in place, which was announced on 19th February 2016. The original action had been decided in favour of the bank (RBS) - but then there was an appeal on three grounds.

To start with the original action, it is valuable to summarise the points raised, and how they were dealt with.

The salesman (this was the first time, I believe, that an ex-swap-salesman has appeared as a witness of fact) described the sales process, the discussions held with Mr Ian Parker, the owner of Crestsign, and discussions and financial considerations with the RBS "Credit Committee".

The most notable financial issue was the substantial size of the "Credit Reserve", sometimes known as "Hidden Line of Credit", or, misleadingly "Contingent Liability" (the understanding is usually that the amount relates to the contingency of breaking the contract, whereas, in that event, the reserve disappears; it is the "contingency of the contract continuing" that is being reserved against.) This, relating to the contract finally sold, was in the order of a factor of ten times greater than the day one profit that RBS made on the transaction. While the profit was in the order of £50,000-£70,000, the Credit Reserve was £640,000 (figures taken from Deputy Judge Mr Tim Kerr QC's lucid judgment).

The only further consideration of the Credit Reserve in the judgment was that RBS had stated that it was an internal figure, not generally provided to any client. However, it merits more attention.

The original agreement proposed a contingent liability for the *loan* of some £300,000. This relates to the portion of Crestsign's assets that RBS was marking down for support if the loan broke any of its covenants. (Remember the covenant mantra – "If things go wrong, we'll take it back, or worse"). Crestsign was effectively committing security over those assets to RBS, as security for its covenants. However, Crestsign had no idea that the product sold to "protect him against interest rate rises" involved a marking down of more than double that amount of assets!

Had Crestsign tried to port the "loan plus swap" combination, any new lender would need to set up a similarly large reserve.

The case turned on the written clauses in the contract, whereby RBS disavowed itself of providing any advice. The legal position, I understand, was whether the relevant clauses were "Basis Clauses" or "Exclusion Clauses". As I am not a lawyer, and can only make a layman's interpretation of these expressions, I have not commented further.

RBS was considered to be adequately protected by these clauses which put all responsibility for losses onto due to the sale to Crestsign.

The evidence of the swap salesman – Mr Nathan Gillard, received some very pointed comments from the judge – Mr Justice Kerr. He was called "a salesman to his bones", which, together with other criticisms, left no doubt as to how the judge viewed him and his evidence.

The appeal was mounted on three grounds:

1) **Whether the Basis clause contained in the bank's standard terms and conditions prevented Crestsign's cause of action against the Banks for negligent advice;**

2) **Whether the information duty owed by the Banks extended beyond explaining the products that the bank decided to offer to informing Crestsign about other products including an interest rate cap;**

   and

3) **Whether the Bank's description of the potential break costs of the swap as "substantial" was an adequate description.**

Again, the legal strength of these arguments is a matter for a lawyer, so I cannot comment definitively – my advice is not legal advice. However, it should be noted that as Crestsign was a company, and assumed to be adequately responsible for making its own decisions, and deciding whether it needed to take professional advice in that regard. But the second and third points look weak to me. Regarding the second, why should a bank *selling to a company* have any duty to describe any other products than one it wants to sell him? If COBS does not apply, there is no duty to consider suitability – only one not to mis-describe.

The third point seems to me to be almost risible. What other descriptions should be used? "Enormous"? "Humungous"? Only the first point appears to have any potential, and only then if the areas where the salesman mis-described the product, or omitted key characteristics, is deemed to be adequately severe and culpable.

However, there is some traction in the second point, if only in reverse. If the point is made that the term "hedging" is a misleading description of the product, then such miss-description may support a challenge to the contract clauses, i.e., point one. The issue is that "hedging" is clearly a literal description of a cap, while swaps involve risks that were not disclosed.

As with other similar cases, the derivative does not appear to be shown in the Crestsign balance sheet – the £3.5 million shown as over 1-year creditors is presumably mainly made up from the loan advance. I understand that auditors must now ensure swaps are included in company balance sheets, irrespective of the size of the company.

However, merely considering derivatives at their market value is only a partial solution. It is like trying to run an insurance company by simply deducting claims paid from premiums received, and treating the balance all as profit. This pretends that the credit reserve ("CEE") above, does not exist. As Warren Buffet stated, "when the tide goes out we will see who has been swimming naked".

8.
HOW THE EX SALESMEN SEE IT

"Men may keep a sort of level of good, but no man has ever been able to keep on one level of evil. That road goes down and down. The kind man drinks and turns cruel; the frank man kills and lies about it."

G.K. Chesterton — *The Innocence of Father Brown*

Most of the former derivatives salesmen seem to have kept a low profile since the heyday of interest rate "hedging" came to an end at the start of 2009. While many of them have retained their roles in some shape or form, within the same bank, or obtained similar roles in other banks (social networks, primarily LinkedIn, are invaluable in investigating this matter); news has been emerging into the public domain to suggest that banks are continuing to promote these products.[16]

Clearly, volumes of lending have fallen, and it is expensive to run a SME swap sales force, so many of these units have probably been downsized substantially, if not broken up. However, this raises other questions. If there was a market for 'protection' when interest rates were about 5%, surely there must be one when they're ½%? Surely, those rates can only go up (although they're obviously taking a long time to do so?). If banks have found a genuine market, surely there should be other ways of reaching it – possibly via lower cost internet selling techniques?

Furthermore, in a depressed economy, one might expect there to be more demand for "hedging" – if money is tighter, unexpected rate rises might be harder to stomach than in a buoyant economy. However, the practice seems to have been wound down substantially, if not actually died.

In order to sell derivatives as 'hedging', it was important for the product not to generate costs for the client at an early stage. At the outset, the likely costs would have been known with a far greater degree of certainty than the later ones. However, working on how the market was pricing and trading these risks, those who designed the products could often design a profitable product, which had zero payments from the client in the starting period (or even payments *to* the client). The detriment was expected to emerge later – and selling on the expected detriment generated the bank profit.

While most ex-swap-salesmen have kept relatively quiet about their activities, at least two of them have now set themselves up as "swaps advisors", and approached both new client borrowers, with the intention of advising them on "hedging "their loans; and also approaching those who complained about mis-selling, in order to promote their reports. Many of those reports contained wording suggesting they were either to be used in court, or to support an applicant in the FCA review.

---

[16] Linkedin provides evidence.

In fact, just two of these ex salesmen have produced a large number of reports for those who have been miss-sold. I am aware that some have been used in court and that at least one ex salesman has appeared in court as an expert witness.

I have reviewed many of these reports, and they can only, at best, be described as variable. My issues are as follows:

- Primarily, judging the acceptability of contracts considered by the profitability to the bank. This is also related to the remuneration of the salesman. The format is that, if a bank makes "too much" profit from a deal, it is unsatisfactory, otherwise it is OK. This ignores the risks.

- While such a test may have met FSA/FCA criteria or otherwise, it is important to note that commercial transactions do not receive any protection from the FCA's "COB" or "COBS". Accordingly, such advice is relatively worthless unless the purchaser had for some reason, the advantage of consumer protections.

- While "reasonable levels of profit" were often cited, there was no reference to publicly available documents, or published standards of acceptable or unacceptable profitability.

- Accordingly, the criticism contained within these reports boiled down in essence to a personal view of "I think the bank made too much profit on this deal".

- Although my knowledge of the law is far from comprehensive, I understand that, other than in very exceptional circumstances, parties may charge what they like in connection with commercial transactions. In particular, a bank providing more than one financial product, might load one, or another to achieve an overall target profitability. Financial institutions, certainly including banks, will measure profitability on a client basis.

- Moreover, it is important to note that what might seem an excessive charging structure is deemed to be regulated by the law of competition – and that if Bank A is charging too much, the client is free to go to Bank B.

–   In other words, "profiteering is not racketeering".

–   The above excludes, of course, the issue of a bank deliberately misleading a client about the nature of or risks within the products they are selling.

–   Other than the above, some of the work provided was highly suspicious. One "advisor" suggested that the borrower asked the bank if he could close out his swap, without checking if such action might affect a subsequent legal claim. The financial justification of this step was also not explained.

–   The format of this advice was often bizarre. As mentioned before, one "report" took the form of a draft letter to the mis-selling bank, couched in language of a particularly low level. "Cor Blimey, we wuz robbed!" would perhaps be going a little too far, but is not that far from the mark. Bearing in mind that the purchaser was a qualified medical practitioner and successful entrepreneur, I shudder to think how he might have defended such wording as his own if examined by a competent barrister.

My greatest objection to such reports is that they never explain the real risks of the products sold – capital risk, collateralisation risk, and creditworthiness risk. This is not surprising, given that discussing these risks would have probably aborted any sale that the ex-salesman advisor had made. He was not, for example, likely to say "buying this product will reduce your creditworthiness with both us and any other bank". The salesman relied on the "non-advisory" nature of his relationship with the client, as covered by the documentation, which provided, and provides, his and his bank's "legal shield" against mis-selling claims. It is strange then, that while taking advantage of this shield himself, the same salesman now holds out that his own expertise is now capable of breaking that same shield.

These salesmen were, and are, licenced to sell derivatives via a CF30 qualification – the FCA's formal permission to sell financial products face to face to clients. Apparently, it gives them consent to sell derivatives, without fully explaining the risks to the clients. I do not know what or how they currently sell.

From an SMEs point of view, it is difficult to visualise any of the products as 'hedging', if that term is taken simply to mean as a reduction in risk. The products simply exchange one risk for others, which are likely to be more insidious, and where the overall interest rate risk, including capital values, is asymmetrical between rate rises and rate falls.

To turn these arguments on their head, one might ask "how would a totally honest and open swap salesman have described those products? My attempt is as follows:

Honest and Open salesman - "This product will give you a cap on your outgoing if interest rates rise. But if they fall, or even the forward curve shape changes, (without current interest rates necessarily falling), both you and the bank are more and more exposed to capital related risks. If these risks crystallise to a severe enough extent, we will blame you for all the damage. Also, the swap immediately mars your ability to refinance with another provider."

Clearly, even a disclosure falling way short of the above would almost certainly deter any borrower, unless they were absolutely desperate for the money. So, the salesmen said nothing of the kind, and the definitions within the bank presentation slides of the risks involved confined themselves to the following two statements:

1) A client would need to pay on a regular basis, while immediate interest rates fell below a certain point, for the duration of that fall, and

2) The product may be subject to a break cost (possibly negative), depending on interest rates at the time.

Other than that, every bank relied upon the blanket clauses contained in the documentation, that the bank was not giving advice to their client (despite heavy descriptions as "hedging", "insurance", and "protection" by the salesmen). Any wording used by that salesman, however misleading or duplicitous, was whitewashed out of the picture by those clauses.

In the next chapter, we investigate the role of the main regulator, the FCA, and other regulators who might have been expected to have an interest in the matter. AS the same individuals who oversaw swap sales at the FSA had transferred to the FCA, it is unlikely that they would be been to take any action which might expose their past behaviour to criticism.

Hence the swap review implemented by the FCA was very much a watered-down version of what was required. Banks could, and did, rig the work in their favour, especially where consequential losses were concerned.

Banks have also been allowed to capriciously impose charges within the process, which, in some cases, cancel out the redress totally. This is particularly prevalent for insolvent companies, where banks have effectively colluded with insolvency practitioners.

Recent "Buzzfeed" revelations show what was going on, and has been concealed by banks, professionals they employ, and regulators.

Other regulators have either been inert, or seen the problem as belonging to other agencies – as in the "Yes Minister" way of doing things.

EXAMPLE
CONNAUGHT PLC - MEARS GROUP PLC - TWO SOCIAL HOUSING CONTRACTORS

Connaught Plc was a FTSE250 company operating in the social housing sector.

According to Wikipedia;

–   Connaught was shaken by a series of events triggered by the abrupt departure of its CEO Mark Davies in January 2010, following the sale of his shares valued at £5.5m.

–   After Connaught issued a positive statement, shareholders were surprised when the business issued a profits warning on 26 June 2010: the company explained that the emergency budget introduced by the new government had damaged the company's profitability.

–   Connaught subsequently warned of a 'material loss' for the year ended 31 August 2010.

–   Mark Tincknell, who had taken over the running of the business again when Davies departed, then resigned as CEO on 8 July 2010 and Ian Carlisle took over the post.

- Sir Roy Gardner was appointed Chairman to Connaught's Board in May 2010, following the departure of chief executive Mark Davies.
- On 8 September 2010, Connaught plc and Connaught Partnerships, the company's social housing arm, were put into administration.

An informed press view of Connaught's collapse can be found on Building.co.uk[17]

Now, Connaught appears to have been overtrading, and overextending itself, which is clearly something that its financial reporting team (heavily PwC weighted) could not be expected to prevent. However, the swaps sold to Connaught seem to provide a clue. See the 2007 accounts, where Connaught, having borrowed £150 million from RBS and their banking syndicate peers, stated:

> "The interest exposure is currently on a 100% floating basis. In 2007/08, we will evaluate the benefits of entering into interest rate hedges to cover a substantial proportion of our core long term debt following the increased level of debt..."

In the 2008 accounts, the deed had been done:

> "During the year we entered into interest rate hedges which fix the Group's exposure to interest rate movements over approximately 70% of our core long term debt."

This merrily ignores the fact that loss through "interest rate movements" is not just on cash flows!

> "The Group's interest rate risk arises from long term borrowings. Borrowings issued at variable rates expose the Group to cash flow interest rate risk. Borrowings issued at fixed rates expose the Group to fair value interest rate risk. Group policy is to maintain approximately 70% of its core long term borrowings in fixed rate instruments."

---

[17] http://www.building.co.uk/the-collapse-of-connaught/5005823.article

This is strictly untrue, as fixed rate borrowings risk (as opposed to swap laden borrowing risk) relates only to revenue, and not capital value. See below.

> "The Group enters into fixed to floating interest rate swaps to hedge the fair value interest rate risk arising where it has borrowed at fixed rates in excess of the 70% target"

Now, my problems with the above are as follows:

1) There is absolutely no reasoning or justification supplied regarding the 70% figure. My impression is that the accounting profession believes that directors should just pluck a figure out of the air. There appears to be no guidance as to where such an important figure should come from.

2) Although the two rate risk sentences are among the best explanations I have seen in any public accounts, they do not recognise the difference between fixed rate loans, and the combination of a variable rate loan plus a fixed to floating derivative. The latter are potentially deadlier legally, but they ae similar financially.

Overall, the term "hedging", while being an industry-accepted term, is ambiguous in that its unalloyed use implies a step away from risk, whereas, of course, such products induce their own risk, often far more treacherous than those abated.

Without full details of the derivatives purchased, Connaught's internal accounts, and negotiations with RBS and other banks, it is difficult to produce a full picture.

However, what I can say is follows:

— Post September 2008, the swaps would have become "cash vacuum cleaners", and been, at least in part, contributors to the "Shoe-box accounting" described by Mr David Costly-White of KPMG Insolvency Practitioners.[18]

---

[18] http://www.building.co.uk/the-collapse-of-connaught/5005823.article

–   There is no mention of the swap that I can find in any of the insolvency proceedings. I suspect RBS quickly effected a break after Connaught's prospects of survival were adequately low, to "bury the bodies".

–   The "Building.co.uk" article above asks why RBS did not extend finance. Apart from RBS's own parlous position, and the need to "feed GRG", the derivatives would have reduced Connaught's creditworthiness by the "CEE" reserve, which could be in the order of ten times the market value of the derivative. They would then be absolutely horrendous as a lending proposition.

–   "Building.co.uk" cites Connaught's rival, Mears, who survived the crash. On page 5 of their 2008 accounts, Mears state:

–   Happily, on a quick check on the 2018 Interim Accounts, the same seems to apply. Mears have not (yet) been tempted by dodgy bank salesmen.

–   "The company does not undertake any trading activity in financial instruments. All activities are transacted in Sterling. The company does not engage in any hedging activities".

–   So, in summary, Connaught were not really "hedging" – *what they were actually doing was undertaking amateur derivative speculation.* They then paid the price.

–   The FRC's announced an investigation into Connaught in 2010. In 2015 and 2016 it disciplined its senior employees and PwC in respect of accounting irregularities in 2009 and 2010. These appear to be minor, and probably have their roots in the problems generated with the help of the swaps.[19]

–   All that we do know about the part the swaps played in Connaught's demise is that it certainly would not have been trivial.

---

[19] https://www.frc.org.uk/Our-Work/Enforcement/Enforcement/Present-cases/Connaught-plc.aspx

9.
HOW THE FCA/PRA (AND OTHER REGULATORS) SAW IT

All it takes for Evil to prevail in this world is for enough good men to do nothing.

Francis Burke

Many SMEs complained to the FSA (as it then was) after the 2008/09 regarding swap mis-sales – these were generally ignored by the (then) FSA, who had decided that, even if sales had been made to private individuals, they were not going to take on the banks. Tony Blair and Gordon Brown had made it clear that banks were a 'protected species', and the FSA contented itself with arranging for minor infractions to be highlighted in the financial press, together with a photograph of Margaret Cole, their then Head of Regulation, which became virtually a weekly event.

However, under public pressure, and that from MPs, notably Guto Bebb, via the House of Commons debate on the subject, the FSA agreed to investigate whether a review was called for.

From the start, the FSA's behaviour was sluggish, and any action was only undertaken begrudgingly. Clearly, any mis-selling that might be discovered would have taken place under their "reign", and subject them to more public and governmental criticism.

The FSA's initial public announcement[20], was significantly misleading, hence it set the tone for an underweight and flawed process. It is worth analysing it by sentence (my comments in italics):

– **Products which aim to reduce risk to interest rate fluctuations have been sold to small businesses.**

The aim of the selling bank was a) to take an extra day one profit by exposing the client to extra risk and b) restrict his ability to refinance.

The client is newly exposed to Interest rate fluctuations by now being financially locked into the forward curve.

This sentence is substantially "pro-bank", and, more worryingly "pro-mis-selling".

– **They are typically sold alongside a business loan from banks.**

They were always sold beside a loan – how else could anyone be exposed to interest rate risk?

---

[20] http://www.fsa.gov.uk/library/other_publications/interest-rate-swaps

The iniquity was that the risks that were linked to the loan covenants were not disclosed.

–   **However, they can vary in complexity and can, therefore, be mis-sold in most cases.**

The complexity of a product is overwhelmingly its exposure to downside risk – i.e., "anything but a cap" is suspect. Any additional complexity is a red herring.

–   **We explain these types of products and if you are entitled to redress if your firm was sold one.**

They do not explain capital risk, or collateralisation risk. Is this because they do not understand them, because they want to be "bank-friendly", or because they are covering up their own past laxity and ignorance?

My understanding is that individuals from the FSA were secretly agreeing levels of profit/commission with banks selling swaps – this, as mentioned earlier, was confirmed by two ex-salesmen who have now turned swaps experts, and another expert in the field. There is supporting evidence for this in the terms the FSA set for the subsequent review – derivative sales were deemed "appropriate" if the break costs would not have exceeded 7.5% in a "pessimistic but plausible scenario". Such an approach was clearly based on residential mortgage rules, but this method of assessment ignored two vital issues:

a)   If the product was sold deceitfully, i.e., by using deliberate mis-descriptions or omissions, then no level of break costs under any circumstances could be acceptable. The regulator was, in effect, trying to publicly sanctify the secret rules described above – probably on the insistence of the banks it was supposed to regulate. This, of course, kept the redress costs down.

   Clearly, this also dumps a major part of the derivative damage (fall in value and CEE, against the client), into the client's balance sheet.

b) The FSA's covert test is a dangerous surrogate for acceptability, bearing in mind the language used to sell these derivatives. The sales scripts were heavily laced with terms such as "hedging", "insurance", and "protection", and the risks deliberately underplayed. To the arguments that "the documents exclude any liability for what we said", I would suggest that, as material risks would have been present in ALL products presented to the client, and would have damaged ALL borrowers in the same way, (though, depending on the borrower, not necessarily to the same extent), and "to the client should have taken advice" ; by not only the fact that the language used disguises any need for advice, but that client detriment exceeds client benefit in every case, and the detriment is more insidious. It is like combining vitamins and poison, and describing the result as "vitamins".

After pressure from MPs, the FSA agreed to set up a mis-selling review for swaps, the operation of this being handed down to the new FCA when the FSA was dissolved. I was told that over twenty drafts of the agreement as to how this should operate were sent by the FCA to banks, and each one returned, re-worded into the form the banks wanted it to take.

The FCA (as it had become) established a test for "sophistication", whereby it deemed it appropriate for firms to be excluded based on turnover, net capital, and number of staff. Such measures are clumsy surrogates for whether the client realised what they were buying – and, in the context of the conduct of the salesmen, inappropriate.

In order to give the process some credibility, a task force of "independent reviewers" was created, provided by large management consultancy/accounting (or legal firms), led by KPMG. This focussed on easily identifiable factors, and came up with five "faults" that indicated a miss-sale:

a) The derivative sold was larger in financial size than the outstanding loan at the time
b) The term of the derivative was longer than that of the loan
c) The derivative was "too complicated for the client to understand"
d) The loan documentation did not insist on "hedging"
e) The client did not express an interest in hedging.

The weakness of such a system, and its "gameability" (i.e., the ability of a bank to hijack it) is only too apparent to anyone who understands derivative risk. Focusing on a) or b) allows attention to be taken away from the risks that were present in such a derivative of ANY size or term. The "complexity" usually referred to either "beefing up" the downside (floor), or options presented against the borrower; e.g., a cancellation option at a certain time or times, granted to the bank. However, the imposition of these were usually accompanied with a reduction in the associated "cap" rate, in order to compensate for the value of the detriment. The banks and the FSA had agreed a formula for profit, this would be simple for an expert to price into the contract, and as such is not as bad as it seems to be painted. However, giving the bank a cancellation option reveals the bank's true motives; – if the bank's intention was REALLY to sell "hedging", why would they want an option for themselves to cancel it? The story starts to fall apart, and reveals sales driven solely by profit and commission motives.

Point d), whether loan documents required "hedging" or not is vacuous – any bank can insist on any contract terms being added to written ones; and the only issue here is whether the borrower was "bounced" into the derivative after he had taken irrevocable steps in connection with the promised loan, such as exchange of contracts. I understand that this was a particularly favoured tactic of RBS, who also had a knack of promising a loan, selling a swap, and then withdrawing the loan offer. Strange as it may seem, such behaviour helps a bank's growth (Goodwin tactics), as the loan ties up capital, whereas the swap (at least, according to sloppy reserving practices at that time) generates more quick profit.

As far as point e) was concerned, if the client was misled by inadequate and misleading descriptions, who wouldn't express interest? However, the question of "whether the client had expressed interest in "hedging"" carried great weight in the FCA review so geared that review more towards bank control.

As most sales were swaps ("Vanilla Swaps", as the banks now insist on calling them), the banks were off to a flying start in being able to either resist any claim, or impose a penal "replacement product".

The next issue with the review was consequential loss. This related to the damage that the derivative sale had done to the business aside from the payments it had generated. This is actually very hard to calculate, in that it is impossible to say with certainly what would have happened if the swap had not been sold.

However, the FCA did two astonishing things. First, it stated that victims would be "put back into the position they would have been if the swap had not been sold". Having made this grandiloquent promise, it then stated that this aim might be achieved by "crediting the swap payments to be refunded to the borrower with a bald 8% simple interest".

The failings of such a simplistic approach are only too obvious. The complexity of assessing the equivalent "no swap" business (or, as lawyers call it, the counterfactual) can be described by the following:

a) Immediately the swap is sold, the borrower becomes less solvent, as the swap represents a debt in his books.

b) The banking industry (and, indeed the derivatives industry as a whole) requires collateralisation of derivatives – that is, a hypothecation if the borrower's assets in case his swap position deteriorates. This was deliberately concealed from the borrower – while the bank "credit committee" marked down a portion of the borrower's assets for this purpose, the bank relied on using the loan covenants to control the borrower, and never disclosed the hypothecation of his assets.

c) Accordingly, the borrower would have become a worse risk to any competing bank for three reasons – the market value of the swap, the collateralisation, and his ignorance of what was going on – far from being "hedged", he had become an amateur derivatives speculator!

d) When the crash happened, the ordinary business activities of the borrower would usually have more become difficult, in any case.

e) Borrowers would realise that what had been sold as "hedging" was in fact a liquidity vacuum cleaner.

f) When the borrower attempted to refinance, the swap would deter other lenders.

g) Borrowers would then become less efficient and focussed as managers, as they were distracted by the unpredictable swap issues.

h) Bank staff would continually lie to swap-inflicted clients as to what was really going on.

i) There is a range of possible outcomes under real scenarios. At best, the client would have had enough of an asset base to withstand the effects of the swap, and possibly buy it out. At worse, he would have become insolvent.

j) Banks, especially those that had been bailed out by the UK government, were "liquidity hungry". They saw no issues with breaking up any company where they had the power to do so, whatever their prospects of survival might have been. Such was the need for capital and liquidity (especially at those when the forward curve fell, and all the nasty swaps suddenly became a lot nastier).

k) As discussed before, weakened clients could usually be forced into "support" units, such as RBS's "GRG", or Lloyds "BSU". Charges could be heaped upon them, and then the coup de grace administered.

Clearly "8% simple interest" is hardly an adequate compensation for all of that!

It is now time to examine the other half of the breakup of the FSA – the PRA. This body was created to promote and ensure bank solvency, and was effectively subsumed into the Bank of England, although it is theoretically a separate body.

The first fly in the ointment was the fact that RBS and much of Lloyds TSB banks were still under public ownership. Gordon Brown had been told that these could be 'flipped' back into the private sector once the fuss had died down. As it turned out, this was more than a little optimistic. Regulators therefore got the coded message that they shouldn't disrupt George Osborne's sales plans. Although Lloyds proved a more attractive sale, the investment community seems to have got wise to RBS.

The second fly was the pressure on regulators to soften down the effectiveness of the swap review – as RBS had sold almost as many as the other three major banks put together, they would be hardest hit by a full review. Accordingly, Martin Wheatly, the FCA's head at the time, directed his energies towards the life assurance and pensions industries. A not uncommon tactic of the omniregulator.

However, with an action that might have justified Harry Palmer's quotation from the Ipcress File – "You were only supposed to blow the bloody doors off" – Wheatly then shocked the life industry and markets by announcing an investigation into, virtually, anything that anyone had ever sold to anyone, back to the year dot.

On the other side of the coin, recapitalisation of the banks was now seen as a top government priority. With capital proving impossible to raise elsewhere, and MP's pressing banks to make new loans, the only place that banks COULD improve their liquidity ratios was to break up customers with existing loans. As those with swaps had extra problems (collateralisation), and by breaking THESE companies up, the collateralisation would disappear, they were the obvious targets. The important aim was to get the company effectively under control (swamped by fees and charges) before cancelling the swap (to prevent any questions from the Insolvency Practitioner) – and then closing down the business.

To use my standard expression, the regulator (PRA/FSA – with assistance from the short-lived Asset Protection Agency) went from supine to vulpine – demanding raises in capitalisation, and not caring where these came from. Bank of England reports discussed "distressed loans" - "non-performing loans" – and "loan forgiveness" (as if the banks were a bunch of Jesus Christs)! Any victim reading these reports would have been left in no doubt whose side the PRA was on.

The recent "Buzzfeed" revelations indicate how RBS's GRG (Global Restructuring Group) operated – clearly with no consideration for whether any of their customers actually recovered, and with the profitability and liquidity generated by the opposite their clear aim. Studying these with the annual reports of the APA clearly demonstrates that this behaviour was sanctioned official practice.

Guto Bebb stated in the February 2016 Commons debate that all of the individuals he encountered when asking questions of the FCA were the same ones he had met at the FSA, and asked the same questions to! Unfortunately, they have brought with them an ignorance of interest rate risk, and an arrogant refusal to even contemplate that they may be in the wrong.

A fixed rate loan victim was told by one of these regulators (a Mr David de Souza) that banks would regard her business as a better risk, as she had borrowed at a fixed rate, rather than a variable one. I have this in writing. This is a clear hangover from the "Gordon Brown Curve" covered in Chapter 6. What is worse, the ignorance is perpetuated in the FCA rules on residential mortgage provision. In the midst of some very creditable research, the FCA apes its predecessor by insisting that the Bank of England Interest Rate Forward Curve is a "Forecast" of interest rates, and should be used in interest rate stress tests to check the future affordability of mortgages if interest rates rise![21]

While stress tests are a good idea, and the size of the stress level, in terms of interest rate increase (1%?, 2%?, 3%?) could be regularly discussed between the regulator and the industry, NO FORWARD CURVE, EVEN THE BANK OF ENGLAND'S ONE SHOULD EVER BE USED AS A FORECAST. The explanations as to the reasons for its weaknesses as a forecasting tool would be far too much to understand for most mortgage advisors, let alone their clients.

For formal confirmation of this, I suggest reading chapter 6 of "The Professional Risk Manager's Guide to Finance Theory and Application (2008)", a PRMIA entry level textbook on the derivatives market, and associated theories. The relevant graphs and explanations are shown on page 184 of that book.

For an empirical illustration, I have researched the history of the forward curve between 2005 and 2015. For every day that the Bank of England publishes the information. I have compared where the curve "keeps its shape" as time advances, and where it "follows its nose", i.e., follows the path it seems to suggest. While for shorter terms (6 months), the two are around equal, as the term lengthens, the "holds its shape" results are far stronger. This suggests

---

[21] Read the FCA's CP 16/10 (185 pages), and CP 10/31 (585 pages), most of which are fine.

that the curve is only of value in short-term projections, and then only arguably. I can make this study available on request.

In my view, the FCA could be sued (unless they have legal escape clauses in their constitution), for misleading at least anyone who opted for a fixed rate before UK rates fell to ¼% post the Brexit vote. I would be happy to provide expert witness advice in any such legal action.

The question then is obviously – if the FCA can use this curve to mislead, why didn't the banks do the same? The answer is – a few of them did, but the forecasts in the slide presentations that were used to sell swaps were maximum two years, and often shorter. Banks clearly employed people with PRMIA qualifications, and they were savvy enough not to incriminate themselves with this schoolboy howler!

At least one bank derivative salesman states on their website "We have advised our regulator, the Financial Conduct Authority (FCA)". One wonders then who is regulating whom.

As far as other regulators are concerned, their attitude seems to be to leave it all to the FCA. The Financial Reporting Council (FRC), who regulate both accountants and actuaries, have only recently acknowledged the risks that companies face if they are mis-sold (or mis-buy ☺) derivatives.

The FRC seems to have a special affinity for banks. Their July 2016 publication, "Corporate Culture and the Role of Boards" is particularly noteworthy for the frequency and prominence of quotations from bankers, and ex bankers. The FRC's own chairman, quite reasonably, provides the one in introduction, but of a total of 42 'Sidebar" quotations, six come from bankers, five from Lloyds Bank executives or directors, and no fewer than four from Mr António Horta-Osório, Chief Executive of Lloyds Banking Group! The banks' message – "We Own Our Regulators" – could not be more stark!

It might well be inferred that the FRC believes that bankers can be held up as cultural examples for other industries. My own experience perhaps implies the polar opposite.

In its September 2014 publication "Guidance on Risk Management, Internal Control and Related Financial and Business Reporting", the FRC states:[22]

---

[22] https://www.frc.org.uk/Our-Work/Publications/Corporate-Governance/Guidance-on-Risk-Management,-Internal-Control-and.pdf

28. Risks will differ between companies but may include financial, operational, reputational, behavioural, organisational, third party, or external risks, such as market or regulatory risk, over which the board may have little or no direct control.

Anyone who has understood the preceding chapters will realise that, if you lock yourself into a derivative, you expose yourself to a whole load of market risk for free – and lose a great degree of control over the solvency of your business!

However, the FRC have now acknowledged derivative risk in their 2015 and subsequent work. In April 2016's "Guidance on the Going Concern Basis of Accounting and Reporting on Solvency and Liquidity Risks", the FRC states:

Sensitivity analysis

5.5 Directors may wish to undertake sensitivity analysis. Sensitivity analysis involves measuring the impact on forecasts of changing relevant assumptions within severe but plausible scenarios and provides directors with an understanding of the critical assumptions that underlie such forecasts. As an example, directors might consider the impact of varying assumptions of future revenue levels on the company's compliance with current financing covenants and the need for future additional financing. The extent of the analysis should be proportionate to the size, complexity, particular circumstances of the company and the risks it faces. It may, depending upon the facts and circumstances, be appropriate to test the impact of changes of all or some of the following:

- ...
- margin requirements dependent on varying underlying prices for derivative contracts;
- ...

Contingent liabilities[24]

5.16 Directors should consider the company's exposure to contingent liabilities. These may include sources of potential cash outflows during the review period relating to legal proceedings, guarantees, margin or other credit support provisions under derivative contracts, environmental costs and product liability.

Example: Exposure to fixed-price contracts and to movements in foreign currency exchange rates may be amongst the most significant risks for a construction company engaged in overseas markets.

[24]   Defined in Appendix A to FRS102 and IAS37 paragraph 10 as (a) a possible obligation that arises from past events and whose existence will be confirmed only by the occurrence of one or more uncertain future events not wholly within the control of the entity; or (b) a present obligation that arises from past events but is not recognised because (i) it is not probable that an outflow of resources embodying economic benefits will be required to settle the obligation or (ii) the amount of the obligation cannot be measured with sufficient reliability.

Swap victims will note that, as Credit Support Annexes were not used by the swap salesmen, the Directors of these companies would have a virtually impossible job to properly manage risk.

Of other regulators, little needs to be said. Although forced or pressurised interest rate swap sales are clearly anti-competitive, the Competition and Markets Authority, or CMA, don't seem to understand, or care. To quote Peter Vicary-Smith, Chief Executive of Which? Magazine, reporting to the Treasury Select Committee, their report into retail banking was "feeble". He then stated, "I always fail to see why banking should be such a different industry".

The Financial Ombudsman's Service, part of the FCA, has been tasked with addressing complaints for cases where the clam is £150,000 or below. I have never seen one of their reports where the full range of derivative risks has been discussed, or any indication that the writer understands even basic risks.

The next chapter discusses the role of lawyers in swaps mis-selling. A number of swap cases have been taken to court, but most of those which went to judgment have failed. Those with decent prospect of success have usually been settled by banks with draconian gagging contracts ("Non-Disclosure Agreements").

Citing LIBOR rigging, or successfully applying to the court to force senior bank managers and directors to face hostile examination in court, have both proven successful tactics in larger cases.

However, a lack of understanding of what actually happened in swap mis-selling has forced many actions to become mired in irrelevant detail. The key issues are sometimes subtle, and therefore need to be fully understood and explained before court action is contemplated.

EXAMPLE
ALLPAY

I spotted this company in the press – I've not had any contact with the directors or any other staff. However, following their progress via their accounts is interesting: they got involved in derivatives, and it's difficult to see how or why. I'll merely lay out the year by year reporting in their annual accounts, together with my comments:

ACCOUNTS YEAR TO 30 JUNE	ACCOUNTANTS	BANKERS	PAGE	CONTENT
2006	Grant Thornton	HSBC	5	Directly describes the swaps as risky, and refers to note 17 to the accounts
			19	Impossible to analyse the derivatives fully unless more information provided.
				I quote Note 17 to the accounts in full, with my comments in italics below
				"The company has entered into two fixed rate range accrual swap transaction in the year."
				"Fixed rate range accrual" is not a formally recognised term. This gives me no idea what they are hooked into.
				"The notional amounts are for £20m and £10m respectively, with fixed interest rates receivable of 6.25% and 5.3% respectively (only when the LIBOR rate is in the range 0% - 5.5%)."
				"Receiving fixed - looks like a "Hammersmith and Fulham" type speculation. Why did Allpay buy these derivatives?"
				"As part of the agreement, a floating interest rate is also payable by the company on the notional amount."
				So, again, looks like they have "fixed receiver" swaps?
				"Both derivatives have quarterly maturity dates which commenced on 28 December 2005 and 28 March 2006 respectively"

ACCOUNTS YEAR TO 30 JUNE	ACCOUNTANTS	BANKERS	PAGE	CONTENT
				*This means quarterly **payment** dates, I assume, unless there are embedded cancellation options we're not told about, in which case Allpay have decided to insure their bank against risk!*
				The smaller second derivative includes a non-callable interest rate floor at 4% for the term."
				So Allpay pays LIBOR or at least 4%? See previous comments.
				"At 30 June 2006, the fair value of these derivatives was a potential liability of £1,303,236"
				Why "potential"? The "fair value" should be the market value - derivatives on this multi-trillion market are priced continuously.
				"We don't know how the £1.3 million figure was calculated. Is it a market quote, or have they done something with potential payments?"
2007	Grant Thornton	Lloyds TSB	5	As above
			19	Note 17 is identical to 2006, except for the following:
				"At 30 June 2006, the fair value of these derivatives was a potential liability of £4,730,201"
				Oops - an increase in negative value of £3.4 million or 263%. Lucky they didn't call it "hedging"!

ACCOUNTS YEAR TO 30 JUNE	ACCOUNTANTS	BANKERS	PAGE	CONTENT
				Note, this occurred prior to the market upheavals of Northern Rock, et al.
				Or it might have been that Allpay/ Grant Thornton found out the correct way to value the swaps.
				You also need to add the CEE on to the market values to indicate the true risk measure.
				"Since the year end, the company has reached a settlement in order to cancel these derivatives, the combined settlement value to cancel these derivatives is £1.5 million."
				Questions as to why Allpay got away so lightly?
				Was a mis-sale admitted? We would need to see the full contracts.
				"In order to pay this settlement, the company has taken out a base rate loan of £1.5 million. (Details of the 5-year loan, and interest rate, provided)"
				So it needed to borrow in order to get rid of its "hedging?"
2008	Grant Thornton	Lloyds TSB	5	Interest Rate Risk (Risk Statements)
				"The company seeks, as appropriate and as far as possible in the light of its cashflows, to fix interest rate exposure."
				Do they mean exposure to PAY-

ACCOUNTS YEAR TO 30 JUNE	ACCOUNTANTS	BANKERS	PAGE	CONTENT
				MENTS (i.e., floating rates), or CAPITAL VALUES (fixed rates)? You can't fix both! This is looking shaky!
			21	*No new information, apart from the fact that the derivatives had been cancelled by 30/6/08, so the liability then was nil.*
2009	Baker Tilly	Lloyds TSB	5	Interest Rate Risk
				As for 2008 – same comment
				The following was added:
				"However, changes to the banking sector's approach to lending over the last year or so has reduced Allpay's ability to fix the interest rate on all outstanding loans at a rate which the company considers to be in its optimum economic interest."
				"As such some loans are now based on a floating rate linked to LIBOR."
				They were lucky to be able to avoid fixed rate loans, which performed badly since 2009.
			18	Note 13 - all loans are floating rate now.
2010	Grant Thornton	Lloyds TSB	6	Interest rate risk - identical to 2009
			24	Note 24 - on 6 July 2010, the company received £905,000 of damages arising from inappropriate advice in respect of a financial matter.

ACCOUNTS YEAR TO 30 JUNE	ACCOUNTANTS	BANKERS	PAGE	CONTENT
				Could be a settlement amount for the £1.3m swaps loss? Draw your own conclusions.
2011	Grant Thornton	Lloyds Bank Capital Markets		No more mention of swaps. Learnt their lesson?

10.
HOW THE LAWYERS SEE IT

"It is a pleasant world we live in, sir, a very pleasant world. There are bad people in it, Mr Richard, but if there were no bad people, there would be no good lawyers."

Charles Dickens - The Old Curiosity Shop

Many lawyers promote services for addressing the swap mis-selling problem.

Go onto the web and enter the words "interest rate swap mis-selling" and a whole raft of advisors will pop up. Some of these will be technical experts, and some will be solicitors. The quality of their services will vary wildly.

The first thing to check with any lawyer is – do they understand what has been sold? I'll give you an example. Imagine you have borrowed some money from your bank at variable rate (say base rate plus 2%). You are interested in investing via, say, the Funding Circle organisation. They provide a service to lend money to small businesses, primarily fixed rate loans. You lend to some small businesses. You are therefore receiving fixed rate interest, and paying variable rate interest. Is this a derivative?

The answer is yes, but it's complicated to explain, so I'll leave it until later. What you want to watch out for is someone who gives you a one-word answer to that question; or who waffles. Many of the people involved in derivatives advice don't know what they're talking about. If they ever end up in court, they will be up against bank barristers, who will have a much easier job than your barrister. Your barrister has to establish a pretty watertight case that the bank did something wrong. The bank barrister only needs to dig a hole in that case. If your guy (or girl) can't ask or answer simple derivative questions, establishing what was wrong with the sale, your case may get dismissed on summary judgment (i.e., the judge thinks it's bound to fail, so doesn't think it's worth hearing in full).

The banks thought the whole business through very carefully in advance; in fact, they anticipated that there might be problems when they designed the products. The sales process would have been rigorously designed – for example, salesmen being told precisely what to say and what not to say. Documentation was carefully structured to the effect that the bank is not giving advice – just providing product.

As an example, see the following judge's summing up of a *hypothetical* swaps mis-selling case, where the bank has won. It relates to the PowerPoint slides shown to the borrower, prior to the derivative sale.

"Both sides accept that the slides describing products were explained in detail. The first product slide described a Swap, where the contract effectively converts the variable rate loan to a floating rate loan. I see no difficulty there. The second product, the Collar, only comes into operation if rates become relatively extreme. In other words, whereas the swap converts the total payment to a single level amount, the collar restricts the cost (to one party or the other) of more extreme interest rate movements. Both products are regularly traded between willing participants in the swaps markets.

While the third product, the Structured Collar is certainly more complicated than either of the others and has attracted criticism from the regulator, its complexities certainly do not put it beyond comprehension, bearing in mind the diagrams provided. The "Cap" level is set lower, clearly providing a greater benefit to the borrower. This is offset by a progressively greater cost on rate falls, generated by the doubling of the actual fall in rates, below a certain level. However, doubling is not a particularly complicated process, and I am sure a competent accountant could explain to (the borrower) what he would pay under various scenarios. Moreover, the total he must pay in the event of severe falls is curtailed by a limit, which is also, in my view, adequately well explained. I therefore find for the bank"

Your argument would clearly need to defeat those shown above, which describes the broad outcome of most interest rate swaps cases to date.

The FSA/FCA review has been of some assistance to smaller victims, who are entitled to the protection of retail legislation (known as COB or COBS – the Conduct of Business Rules which the regulators impose on product sales and other activities). These are a set of rules and principles, and the derivative sales generally broke so many of these that a court case should be a pushover. However, in my view, it is always worth getting a lawyer involved, for the following reasons:

a) Many bank staff dealing with these cases have no idea of the real iniquity in derivative sales, so the process can be 'the blind leading the blind'. A suitably aggressive lawyer might be able to extract a preferential deal in such circumstances.

b) Lawyers are essential in obtaining 'standstill' agreements. The law is very particular about how long one is allowed to bring a claim, after the event complained about. Even if you are only vaguely considering a claim, you must consult a lawyer about deadlines at the earliest opportunity. I have heard stories of documents hand delivered at 5.25pm on the deadline day – five minutes later, and it would have been too late. This may seem counter-intuitive, but it is the law!

c) Lawyers have good contacts with other essential professionals – barristers, experts and ATE (After the Event) insurance providers. The last ones are the most important. If you go to court, you need to be sure you aren't going to be landed with the bank's legal costs if you lose. ATE insurers will underwrite this loss for you (at a cost, taken from your "winnings" if you win), but this is the main hurdle you need to surmount. After that, the bank will start to take you seriously.

One thing that I have learnt from personal experience is that if you think you have a valid claim, any bank staff you negotiate with in these matters should not be trusted one inch. It is painful to say so, but it does appear that they have hidden agendas (or sometimes not so hidden agendas) to disclose the absolute minimum of information, spin things along for as long as possible, and to try and wear you out. The use of informal negotiation is simply seen as an opportunity to delay.

As a corollary to this, it may be in your interest to "keep the claim alive", slowly maintaining legal action under the radar, while arranging matters such as finance, to your advantage. Again, your lawyer will advise.

d) Lawyers have a clarity of thinking, and the ability to argue cogently and persuasively. The latter qualities obviously would generally apply more to barristers, but not exclusively – however, do not underestimate the value of well-reasoned and powerfully delivered argument, whether written, oral, or both, whoever delivers it. Many cases have been decided on the skill of the advocate, even if a prior assessment of the case might have suggested the opposite.

Oddly, the better prepared you are to go to court, the less likely you are to have to do so. If banks behave as described above, and if you have a good case, they will be keen to avoid going to court. If the real ills of derivative mis-selling are aired in a proper investigative forum, (and not, as in the FCA process, by a ragbag of management consultancy account-ants and junior lawyers), the full truth will emerge. The hedging banks still fear the risk that this will happen.

e)   Unless your case is summarily dismissed, you will be granted what lawyers call discovery. That means that you can see all the records which the bank holds about your case. The most interesting of these show how the bank and their superiors, laughed at the plight they were putting their clients into. I have heard phrases that would make you blench, and would give the press and media a field day. There is no way that any bank is going to let this damaging information get out into the public domain; not only because the media would make hay, but also because they could face some pretty tough questioning in the witness box. This knowledge facilitates a reasonable settlement.

The worst of these is a sixteen-word statement extracted from a tele-phone recording which, it is estimated, cost the bank over £40 million to cover up. £2.5 million a word!

There's also the prospect of all the LIBOR rigging quotations being given a public airing, or of getting a 'whale' (a big hitting high profile bank executive) into court. Banks would do anything rather than let that happen.

However, I have read through a lot of "pleadings", as they are called, and I'm not sure that the full arguments have been brought out in any of the public ones that I've seen. Of course, if any lawyer has the "knockout blow" arguments, they would be inclined to keep it to themselves, and reap the benefits. Inevitably, I'm also sure that, if any bank was presented with such arguments, they would immediately offer to settle handsome-ly, with the usual "hush-hush" (non-disclosure) clauses.

At the time of writing, the "PAG vs RBS" summing up has just taken place, which seems the clearest exposition so far of the duplicity involved in selling interest rate swaps in conjunction with variable rate loans and carefully restricted disclosure.

In brief, the major wrongdoing by the banks is their deliberate failure to disclose the major and ubiquitous risks inherent in selling a swap (or other "derivative with downside"), some of which are incapable of being quantified by any external expert. Slides used in sales presentations show clearly that these risks were deliberately excluded.

The capital issues were far greater than the mere disclosure that "if the client decides to break the contract, there may be substantial break costs (or profits). It is like comparing tennis and boxing. Whereas in a tennis match, where you expect to play until one or the other side achieves a win according to purely numerical rules - with boxing the "game" can be stopped at any time – and the bank, having far greater resources and "professionals" such as Insolvency Practitioners in tow, effectively acts as the umpire, as well as a contestant. Citing covenant breeches is probably enough for a bank to get its own way, and, failing that, the bank simply piles more and more charges on the weakened client; (who, as we have discussed before, cannot refinance), until he is forced to give up.

In the event of a downturn, falls in gross national production, and asset and property values, fall, there is a squeeze on liquidity; so, to stimulate the economy the Bank of England cuts interest rates. This is "Government Hedging", for your benefit. BUT, if a bank has sold you a derivative with downside ("DWD"), you then forego the benefits of Government Hedging, and effectively *bet against the Bank of England.*

This last point is a questionable legal argument, as it could be argued it is either common knowledge, or knowledge that is easily available. However, when a bank uses a description, it carries credibility. So, for example if Barclays calls it hedging, the man in the street would think it was hedging, as he would understand it.

To use a technical term, banks were guilty of "misleading synecdoche". Synecdoche is where a part of something is used to describe the whole, or vice versa – for example, one might say "Boots on the ground" when you meant "sending troops into Iraq" – or, alternatively, one might say "the Americans won the gold medal", when one means the American rowing crew.[23]

In the world of derivatives, as in other fields of expertise, one often uses synecdoche. I noted an example used by a QC (Queens Council – a senior barrister) recently, where he used the term "swaps" as a generalisation for all

---

[23] To be really accurate, it should read "The British Rowing crew!

types of fixed interest derivatives. This usage is common – I have used it myself, and our website is called www.bankirsa.com, where the "irsa" stands for "interest rate swap agreements". We cover other mis-sold interest rate derivatives, as well as swaps.

The term 'hedging" is also used by experts, and herein the problems lie. While the layman interprets "hedging" as moving away from risk, the derivatives community uses the expression more generally, as a derivative one is discussing or promoting. However, this expression is particularly dangerous to the uninitiated, as it conceals the detriments involved in those products (except caps). While the "headline detriments": are revealed - the need to make regular payments to the bank if the current interest rate falls to a certain level - the capital value and associated effects are deliberately concealed.

There is a problem of integrity if this synecdoche is deliberately used to mislead, which in many of the sales scripts and presentations I have seen, it clearly was.

The next chapter looks at the part that accountants played in swaps mis-selling. Due to the technical requirements and complexities of "Hedge Accounting", and also the relaxed requirements of reporting for smaller companies, dangerous swaps were often ignored in published accounts. Even now, when the market value of any derivative needs to be disclosed, the reporting of derivatives in accounts can seriously understate the risk. Accordingly, as I also state elsewhere, the appellation "True and Fair" shown in accounts could read "True and Fair…but Useless" where derivatives are involved.

EXAMPLE
URBAN LIME V NATIONWIDE COMMERCIAL – TAILORED BUSINESS LOANS

Nationwide Commercial holds itself out as being an 'ethical' lending organisation, and Urban Lime is a commercial property developer.

Nationwide Commercial persuaded Urban Lime to take out a 30-year fixed rate bridging loan, in connection with a specific property. Z made it clear that it would not provide any development finance, subsequent to the initial period.

The loan was effected in November 2007. This was a time when the forward curve showed a particularly negative slope. The loan was low start, commencing at 4.78% for 2 years, then reverts to 6.24% per annum. Base rate was 5.75% at this time, and did not fall below 5% until October 2008. On the face of it, a good deal.

The lender granted itself a unilateral break on 1 January 2015, about 7 years from issue (known as a "European" option). Without this option, it would be hard to describe this contract, on the face of it, as a 'derivative 'contract.

A "derivatives expert" has written a report saying that the contract 'contains' a derivative (and is not referring to the European option).

I have just written up an expert report on the current levels of break costs on 25 and 30 year fixed rate loans taken out in the early nineties. Derivatives do not even get a mention – they do not need to. Yet, the essence of those loans and this one is the same. Fixed, regular payments, and break costs linked to the fixed interest rate market.

I would think that most judges would, in the absence of other evidence, throw this one out. Fixed rate loans secured on property are not treated as derivatives in law. Prior to around 1970, virtually all loans (and certainly domestic mortgages) were fixed rate. However, each of these newer contracts needs to be looked at separately. Some of the clauses specifying how to calculate the break penalty are ridiculous.

But, there is a very interesting factor in this case – a clause in the loan agreement (which is primarily for a variable rate loan) is as follows:

"2.3 So as to satisfy Nationwide Commercial (the lender) as to the ability of the Borrower to be able to pay the interest, prior to drawdown Urban Lime (the borrower) must either have accepted a Fixed Rate under clause 8.4 or have assigned to Nationwide Commercial an acceptable hedging transaction"

This statement is quite incredible, due to the following:

If a fixed rate is chosen, the bank plans to sell the difference as a capital sum to a big four bank (I have the name). As Nationwide Commercial makes a profit (hidden from the borrower) on this part of the deal, is shows that the swaps market believes, on that date, that the borrower is taking on a net additional risk. Accordingly, all banks, and bank regulators will see Urban

Lime's business as being MORE risky due to the fix being imposed.

Clearly, the same applies (and it's actually worse) if a fixed to floating derivative is chosen.

Where Nationwide Commercial are exposed is where they say:

> "So as to satisfy Nationwide Commercial as to the ability of the borrower to be able to pay the interest...".

IF THE ABOVE MARKET AND REGULATOR, EFFECTIVELY THE LENDING UNIVERSE, SEE THE BORROWER AS RISKIER, THEY MUST BE *LESS* ABLE TO PAY THE INTEREST!

This statement would be very difficult to justify to a court, with adequate informed and competent expert advice.

11.
HOW THE ACCOUNTANTS SAW IT

After a moment's silence, he added, 'I suppose the hardest thing is to convince anybody that 0+0+0=0. Men believe the oddest things if they are in a series'

GK Chesterton – The Scandal of Father Brown

One of the key requirements of swap mis-selling, is to conceal the damage that the product is capable of doing, for as long as possible. Derivatives can often be created with exactly this purpose in mind, and, in fact, this was almost the genesis of the "Structured Collar" - vilified by Martin Wheatly, for being "too complicated to understand", but whose complexity served a different purpose than simply to confuse the buyer.

Unfortunately, if there is a swap in the books, the usual accountant's certification – "True and Fair" – should be changed to "True and Fair – but Useless", or "True and Fair for Accountants – but not for Bankers".

The usual medium for a company's shareholders to assess the riskiness of a company is the Annual Report and Accounts. Accordingly, the swap salesman's job was to fool the accountants, as well as any other person responsible for buying the derivative on the company's behalf. This could be achieved by persuading the external auditor (and any company accountant) to use or accept the following types of expression:

"The directors have determined that 70% of their borrowings should be hedged by using fixed rate to floating rate derivatives".

"The Company does not speculate in derivatives."

"The **** contract has been designated by the directors as a cash flow hedge"

"The Directors intend to hold *** hedge to its maturity"

Such expressions indicate that the directors, in fact, probably do not know what they are talking about. The following expression explains things in a nutshell:

"Accountants see fixed rates as hedging – banks see fixed rates as risk".

It proved surprisingly easy for bank salesmen to shunt derivatives onto their borrowing clients' balance sheets, often then recorded at zero value. This was due to a misinterpretation of the "hedge accounting", and the "accountant's fallacy".

Hedge accounting is a process which was designed to prevent the need for too many accounting entries, where risk professionals bought equal, but opposite contracts. As such, it makes perfect sense. What is problematic is the use of the term "hedging", where the products bought introduce new risks, as well as containing current ones. When the new risks are in reality unmanageable by the purchasing company, the term "hedging" is called into doubt.

The "accountant's fallacy" was as follows:

"The company" has taken out a variable rate loan, whose capital position I show as total loan capital less any repayments made. It is then exposed to interest rate (cash flow) risk. The derivative, the significance of which I do not fully understand, is supposed to "hedge" the loan, that is, to reduce its risk in some way. Its cash flow features then offset, to some degree, the risk above.

Any payments from or to the derivative I should book as positive or negative interest payments – that's clear.

As far as the capital position is concerned, I want to be prudent. **Therefore, I am not going to reduce the capital amount of the loan shown**. I will show the value of the loan, plus derivative as the loan value. (The derivative value is therefore shown as nil). Therefore, I will be being prudent."

The above reasoning ignores not only the negative value of the derivative at any time, but any consideration of collateralisation. The latter reduce the creditworthiness of the borrower in a way that any bank would recognise, and would repel any alternative lender. However, most accountants are unlikely to understand, and therefore not support any measure in the balance sheet to allow for this. They've been had.

New accounting rules now require that the market value of any derivative be shown in the balance sheet. However, the market (or "fair") value does not fully reflect the risk inherent in the swap.

Any bank looking at the swap sees a collateralisation need of, perhaps, ten times the swap value. This is a serious detriment to refinancing. However, this damage to creditworthiness is not recognised, even under the new accounting rules.

Accordingly, if we have two otherwise identical companies, both with variable rate loans, and one has a swap as well, the "swap –blighted" company is likely to have substantially impaired creditworthiness compared with the other.

The most important issue with accountants, is how unwilling they were to actually do anything about derivative mis-selling, when their charges became riskier, and successive annual accounts failed to highlight that risk. (This is not a criticism of smaller firms, who would not have realised what banks were up to.)

The reasons were this:

1. Accounts are usually drawn up once a year. They often take six months to prepare. That means by the time anything hits the accounts, it is between six and eighteen months out of date.

It can be reasonably stated that events which move the market values of derivatives significantly are rare – but consider the following real-life example:

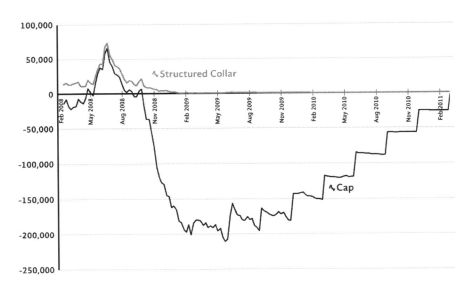

The graph shows a real-life derivative sale, made in February 2008, by a Barclays lady. The black line shows the actual progress of the fair value of the derivative. (The grey line shows how the value of a "vanilla cap" would have progressed over the same time.)

What is most interesting is that the "fair value" of the derivative when it was sold was just minus £15,000! This consists of £14,000 benefit value, and £29,000 of detriment, again, priced on the sale date. But disclosing the bald amount of £15,000 conceals dramatically a high volatility profile – rising to plus £68,000 in June 2008, falling to minus £5,000 in September 2008, rising to plus £9,000 in October 2008, then minus £201,000 by February 2009 – AND THIS WAS ONLY A THREE YEAR TERM PRODUCT! I would defy anyone to have been able to predict the future value pattern of capital loss over the term of the product, by looking only at its history.

What IS more predictable, but makes things a lot worse, is the "hidden line of credit' or "CEE", which the bank needs to reserve for "in case things go wrong". Using the 2% Notional per year of term" assumption, sample adjustment to the above become:

A worsening of £240,000 on day 1 – total negative £255,000 (as opposed to £15,000)!

A worsening of £142,000 in February 2009 – total negative £343,000 (as opposed to £201,000)!!

The CEE 'damage' decreases continually as the outstanding term and the notional amount (in this case) reduce. It is zero at the end of the contract (as is the market value).

Larger companies might draw up accounts more frequently. But even smaller companies need to chart their current position frequently. This is usually done via cash flow analysis – if the company's cash flow is OK, then the company is deemed to be OK. Since the advent of derivative mis-selling (or "miss-buying", to use the ICAEW's neologism) with loans, this is manifestly no longer the case.

If you are drawn into being sold a derivative with "downside" (i.e., the ability to lose you money if interest rate expectations change) included, you can expect the party on the other side of that deal to be checking the market several times a day – perhaps continuously. Bank traders with open positions (i.e., where they are exposed to risk of loss) will focus on those positions intensely, and will bail out, or take other preventative action, if the market moves too much against them. To leave an open position unattended for any length of time would be regarded as dangerous, and losses driven by such negligence would result in discipline or dismissals.

2. The second reason is the advent of "Hedge Accounting". On its own, there is no particular problem with such a concept – that if the characteristics of two financial instruments offset each other, and the quality of that relationship may be used to reduce unnecessary accounting entries and abbreviate required disclosures.

There are two problems here – both with perceptions, rather than any set of rules defining 'hedge accounting'.

The first is that there is a misconception that it is universally acceptable to define fixed interest rates, or rates converted to fixed, as 'hedged'. This was commented on in the previous chapter.

Many accountants clearly accept this misconception. This can be seen by reviewing their glossy brochures on 'hedge accounting'. A universal statement is as follows:

"Company A has decided to take out a fixed to floating derivative in order to manage[24] its interest rate risk".

A bank would (in reality) see this statement as nonsense. To a bank, fixed rates are risky, and floating rates are hedging.

As banks determine the creditworthiness of most SME's, it is worthwhile listening to what they REALLY think (and NOT what their swap salesmen tell you).

This is reflected in the fact that each bank *in its own Annual Report and Accounts* reports variable rate loans at face, and fixed rate loans as a discounting of the total future payments under the loan, whether representing interest or capital. In the second case, this is done by effectively pretending it is a variable rate loan (booked as above), plus a fixed-to-floating rate derivative, which it books at a profit (because the level of fixed rate is obviously set so that the bank makes a day one profit on the swap element).

So, for a fixed rate loan, a bank might record a significant gain or loss over a period, even though all repayments have been repaid on time. This raises

---

[24] The word "manage" is also highly misleading. In most cases, it is **actually surrendering control of the ability to manage the financial aspects of the business in any meaningful way**, until the swap expires. It is probably generated by listening to the sweet exhortations of the bank salesman, rather than applying any logical thought.

the ghastly spectre in that, by hard selling a derivative or fixed rate variant in addition to a variable rate loan, the bank has pulled a fast one. Close examination of the loan's break conditions, and how much ability the bank has to "tweak" these, should provide the answer.

If the fixed rate on a loan exceeds the market swap rate, then the bank can record an instant profit on the sale, and it might be perceived that the sum of the values of "bank plus borrower" increases by this profit. No such profit (or "loss", from the borrower's point of view) accrues for variable rate loans.

I understand the relevant FRS102 accountancy rules have been reviewed more than once, and may be still under review. Prior to that, risky derivatives might never have appeared in accounts, especially for small businesses.

Many lecturers and advisors make much of this market risk related profit – they use it in explaining how interest rate swaps can profit companies. If company A pays x% for fixed rate loans, and y+n% for variable rate loans; and company B pays x+m% for fixed rate loans and y% for variable rate loans, etc, etc, then they can set up a swap between themselves and save some money on what the bank sells, etc, etc. Look some up under "interest rate swap" on Youtube.

It also gives the impression that you can get something for nothing; and as before, the idea is totally wrong.

It makes the assumption that the differences in rates relate purely to profit margin. In fact, they are likely to represent risk loadings, to allow for the fact that company B represents a bigger risk than company A. Therefore, if company A ties its fortunes into those of company B, it exposes itself to higher risk than if it did if its deals directly with the bank. That is the "Credit Risk", which cancels out the profit from the market risk reduction.

If you asked any of these advisors about this they would probably get defensive, and say that this is all hypothetical, they were providing information at an elementary level, anyway you could learn all about risk later in your education. However, this fact is not covered in their videos. One of them has produced a video "what Interest Rate Swap mis-selling is All about", which completely misses the point, and makes the same mistakes many journalists make. "No-one told them what would happen if interest rates went down" a) not strictly true – they were told about cash flow issues, to a degree that would satisfy most judges, and b) ignores the capital and collateral implications.

Accountants are not allowed, per se, advise on derivatives – but that should not mean that they can ignore the risks.

To illustrate the issues concerning disclosure, consider the following two hypothetical statements :

a)   The directors hold xxx derivative for hedging purposes, and intend to hold it to its expiry, and

b)   The directors hold xxx derivative, which currently has a market value of minus £750,000. The directors are aware of the risks of holding this product, and intend to sell it immediately if its negative value exceeds minus £1,000,000.

Company a) will certainly find its creditworthiness degraded in the banking world, due to both the derivative, and their attitude towards it. Unable to rebroke their loans, they will be at the mercy of their lending bank, (who is also their derivative counterparty), and prone to be forced into a "GRG' type unit at short notice.

If you were looking to invest in one of these companies, which would you choose - a) or b)?

Misreporting derivatives has been picked up by the regulator FRC – see the MBS/Grant Thornton case:[25]

Interestingly, on page 5 of the judgment, we find the comment:

20. MBS entered into interest rate swaps to mitigate this risk. The interest rate swaps purchased by MBS were straightforward products. Most of the swaps were Bermudan Options, which meant that the parties could exercise break clauses at defined periods prior to the maturity date. From 2006 to 2012 MBS was a party to around 50 swap agreements with periods ranging between 3 years and 50 years.

---

[25] https://www.frc.org.uk/News-and-Events/FRC-Press/Press/2015/June/Outcome-of-disciplinary-case-against-Grant-Thornto.aspx

The description "Straightforward" merits closer consideration. Compare, for example, the PPF's note on Pension Protection Fund Consultation: Guidance for the Bespoke Investment Risk Calculation.[26]

Here it states, for example:

> 5. We expect that schemes with swaptions should approach investment advisers to do this calculation. Do you agree that this is appropriate, given the complexity of the stress calculation for swaptions?

Swaptions are essentially swaps with an option or options at various dates to get into or out of the swap – which is what adding the Bermudan option did for the MBS swaps.

The answer is that although the mechanics of the derivative are simple, its financial consequences, in terms of capital and collateralisation, are anything but simple. If applying pension fund techniques, in themselves complex, to the evaluation of risk hedging is a complex process when those instruments are involved, a simple statement in the accounts is unlikely to do justice to those risks. The bugbear is market risk, which damages the company that thinks it is just "hedging".

I have read a number of bulletins provided by major accountancy firms on "hedge accounting", and they are strangely quiet on market risk. One wonders if they are trying promote the use of derivatives, and unconscious bias prevents them from addressing the downside.

For a last quotation, look at Wikipedia[27] where it states:

> Interest rate swaps expose users to many different types of financial risk. Predominantly they expose the user to market risks.

A previous version reads:

> Interest rate swaps expose users to interest rate risk and credit risk.

---

[26] http://www.pensionprotectionfund.org.uk/DocumentLibrary/Documents/investment_risk_consultation_May11.pdf

[27] https://en.wikipedia.org/wiki/Interest_rate_swap

> Market risk: A typical swap consists of two legs—one fixed, the other floating. The risks of these two components will naturally differ. Newcomers to market finance may think that the risky component is the floating leg, since the underlying interest rate floats, and hence, is unknown. This first impression is wrong. The risky component is in fact the fixed leg and it is very easy to see why this is so.

Perhaps the change was due to the "Hammersmith and Fulham" mis-selling, where the hapless buyer was locked into interest rate rises over the short term.

The Wikipedia link leads to the Federal Reserve Bank of Chicago's website[28] which provides a fuller picture.

Accountants who want justification for what I have written above should speak to either any actuary, or one of their colleagues involved in final salary pension scheme auditing. I welcome any correspondence on the above.

The accounting profession, via the "Big Four" and other large accountants, made probably hundreds of millions of pounds by assisting banks in various roles – Insolvency Practitioner, Business Report Advisor, or Independent Reviewer (or "Skilled Person") under the FCA review. This appears from my investigations to have been earned by ignoring anything other than cashflow.

The final chapter reviews how the senior judges may view the interest rate swap issues described within this book. This sums up the previous work, and indicates what our finest legal minds may make of a well-constructed case.

EXAMPLE
SISTERS N AND BARCLAYS BANK

The Ns were two elderly sisters who had inherited their father's business in the leisure industry. They recited their business memories and experience, including having to do the washing up for the catering arm of the business at the age of fourteen. No silver spoon introduction to the business world for them.

---

[28] https://chicagofed.org/publications/understanding-derivatives/index

The Ns ran a successful partnership for many years, but, as with many businesses, things were not always plain sailing – weather damage hindered their business, and the Barclays provided support here.

Many of the "usual suspect" names have cropped up in connection with the hard sale of the first swap. The Ns were then sold the second structured collar by Louise Millward of Barclays's Treasury Management nearly two years later. Louise was not qualified to sell until two months after she sold the first derivative.

The first sale was a Structured Collar effected on 11 November 2005.

Structured Collar 2 was effected on 15 October 2007 – The Ns understood this to replace the first one, but in fact U left the first one open, exacerbating the risk to the Ns.

Louise qualified as a "CF30" (i.e., certified by the FSA, now FCA) to sell swaps on 1 November 2007. This appears to be a breach of FSA rules.

KPMG was their auditor, the IP, dictated the manner of the property sale, and audited the purchaser of the property – clearly no conflict of interest there, then! According to The Ns, he appears to have bounced through the sale of one of their sites.

I have received a five-page document from the sisters, detailing their experiences with Barclays. I have quoted the last paragraph, with some slight adjustments to avoid identification.

"We went through a hard time building up the business up until we had three sites. We had a flood that destroyed (one site) and N had a major car crash where two people died, but none of them can compare to the stress and strain this has caused."

The Ns have received advice from an ex-salesman expert – but this "advice" is muddled and opaque. It primarily consists of a string of questions and, as usual, does not cover the capital and collateralisation risks.

12.
HOW THE SENIOR COURTS MAY SEE IT

"Being able to act intelligently and instinctively in the moment is possible only after a long and rigorous education and experience"

Malcolm Gladwell — Blink: "The Power of Thinking Without Thinking"

First, it is worth examining the swaps cases that have gone to court, and therefore have helped to put valuable information into the public domain:

CASE	DATE(S)	OUTCOME (FOR BORROWER)
Guardian Care Homes/Graiseley Properties vs Barclays Bank (Now Lloyds Bank)	Settled April 2014	Settled out of court – settlement rumoured to be in tens of millions of pounds – not unlikely, bearing in mind the size of the claim.
Grant Estates (Scotland)	August 2012	Plaintiff (Pursuer) lost
Green and Rowley[29]	Appeal October 2013	Out of time – appeal failed for the same reason. Swap sold by a junior employee.
Nextia	December 2013	Decided in RBS's favour
Crestsign vs RBS	Settled out of court February 2016	Lost in first instance (initial trial). Case settled prior to appeal hearing.
Holmcroft vs Barclays, KPMG and the FCA	February 2016	Decided in the FCA, etc. favour
Thornbridge vs Barclays	December 2015	Decided in Barclay's favour
LWCP vs RBS	May 2017	Settled out of court - £20 million claim
Opal vs RBS	August 2017	Settled out of court - £670 million claim
PAG vs RBS	March 2018	Appeal Dismissed

It is difficult to form an overall judgment of these cases, although lawyers will

---

[29] The treatment of the derivatives in the company's accounts is of interest. These are available for a small charge from the government website wck2.companieshouse.gov.uk. I can provide an analysis in request.

tell you that "each case turns on its points" – i.e., you have to examine all the details of any case, in order to determine the result. On the other hand, lawyers have "leading cases" - the ones where a senior judge gives a ruling, and this is used as an example to guide cases in the lower courts.

Anyone who has read the previous chapters of this book will realise that all information need to be considered. For any case, the full details of emails, other documents; telephone calls and meeting transcripts, will need to be examined for misleading statements. It is also important to consider the general issues that may have made pretty well ALL sales of derivatives adequately misleading, bearing in mind the omissions, to count as negligent, if not fraudulent, misrepresentation.

Many judges might shrink from delivering such judgments. However, there is a precedent – the UK's first swap mis-selling scandal, which occurred around 1988 – 1991.

In brief, bank salesmen approached local authorities, most notably the London Borough of Hammersmith and Fulham and induced them to specu-late against interest rates. Local Authorities were chosen because they had substantial and secure rate (council tax) income, and rate raising powers that could be relied on "if things went wrong".

A falling yield curve was used as the sales tool – does this sound familiar? The trick was to lock the local authority into paying the VARIABLE rate, and receive the FIXED rate. The sales pitch (and this is the only way it can work) is to demonstrate only the falling part of the curve (which actually RISES in the early years), then sell a contract which expires before the drop kicks in.

An investigation was instigated by Howard Davies, (ironically, now Sir Howard Davies, and Chairman of RBS, who sold the most swaps of all in the current debacle), on, apparently, being told by the then Chief Executive of Hammersmith Council, in June 1988 - "I really wouldn't worry about this, Howard – everyone knows that interest rates are going to FALL" – the standard line fed for the mug to parrot.

By August 1988, Hammersmith had a capital exposure of £4.2 billion, which represented ½% of the total world market in derivatives! In effect, this was an absolutely enormous bet on the future of UK interest rates.

Hammersmith got it wrong. Interest rates rose. The local authority and council taxpayers got stuffed (to use bankers' parlance). Its losses by 1989 were £300 million, representing £4,000 for every council tax-payer!

Anyone who understands the forward curve will know that it DOES NOT represent "where the City thinks interest rates are going to go". This is known as the "pure expectations theory"; (I am not sure if it merits the definition of "a theory"), and while it may work for very short terms (and not even always then), it does NOT predict, or give a "City opinion" of, "where interest rates are going to go". This can be demonstrated both in theory and empirically.

A simple example should suffice to demonstrate this. If I want to maximise my return, I invest where the curve is highest. Let's assume the annual rates are as follows:

For 3 years, 4% pa - For 4 years, 5% pa, - For 5 years, 4% pa.

Clearly if I think backwards, and say "How much do I need to invest to get back £100 at the end of the term? Clearly, it's cheapest to go for 4 years. Does this represent a sensible choice?

Curiously, after a year, I find that the term rates are *still* the same:

For 3 years, 4% pa - For 4 years, 5% pa, - For 5 years, 4% pa.

The reason for this is that the market thinks in terms of DURATION, and not calendar time. In other words, the pattern of rates you see is very likely to look the same as it does today – especially if no new significant information comes into the market. That is, the market doesn't care about future *dates* – what it cares about is the *distance* into the future. So your "clever choice" isn't really clever, after all!

Hammersmith and other local authorities, (and the poor old ratepayers) were saved from their substantial speculative losses by the House of Lords, who ruled that all derivative sales were illegal, as councils were speculating on interest rates, and therefore not "hedging" in any legitimate way. The legal actions extended for some years, especially as some derivatives sold to councils had gone the "right way" (i.e., made money for the council), and made a profit; therefore, the banks wanted this profit back. Ultimately, the banks wrote off £600 million of what were regarded as ill-gotten gains.

Most curiously, the judge involved in the case was a family judge, as the other courts had a major backlog of cases at that time. The law is the law. The judgment was regarded as sound.

In the same was as for Hammersmith, the courts will need to go back to fundamental principles. Can it be right to have a sales force copiously describing a product as "hedging", when the banking community, regulators, and that bank itself regards it as *reducing* the buyer's creditworthiness?

The simple way to avoid misleading behaviour, would have been for banks to insist that a Credit Support Annex (CSA) be used for every sale. If this had occurred, there would, I believe, have been little, if any, mis-selling, and that which did occur would have been easily handled by the Courts. Banks, have, however, chosen to interpret the non-compulsory nature of the CSA as a green light for non-disclosure of the universal and fundamental risks introduced by the derivatives sold – the concealed effective raising of the loan covenant hurdles (the "CEE" that each bank set against the client), and the ample evidence that banks continued to conceal the extent of the derivative detriment during the maelstrom following the 2008 crisis, when banks effectively treated their clients with contempt, to be used as necessary.

The ex-swap salesmen who have now set themselves up as experts would, I also believe, have a lean time of it if they entered a witness box today and were subjected to even mildly hostile examination (questions). The question "you sold derivatives – what is the difference between what you sold, and what we are considering now? " I saw a swap ex-salesman asked this in practice in a conference interview (a conference of Insolvency Practitioners, ironically enough), and his response was "Well, Brian, I set up Pravda Hedging in order to advise companies that had been miss-sold swaps, etc, etc", which completely ignored the question.

If pressed further, our ESS (ex swap salesman) would tell you that "he always obeyed the rules", which meant apply the "FSA test" ("20 basis points per year", the inappropriateness of which I have already described in chapter 8). For a junior operative, this might be a reasonable answer, but for someone who holds themselves out as an expert – to endorse their own past behaviour, untrammelled, requires a "special" level of integrity.

Skilled examination by barristers, and the merits of full disclosure, should put the judges in an adequately strong position to view all of the facts fully. The quality of judgments in the senior courts are renowned. As any judgment (except the most senior) may be subject to appeal, judges are careful to set out their reasoning fully and clearly. The result is so different from the outpourings of "skilled persons", or any of the alphabet soup of regulators who consider that their pearls of wisdom are above their grateful recipients, and so those recipients should not dare to venture forth the view that they are being told a load of nonsense. Typical are the "Final" judgments of the Financial Ombudsman, which I regard as among the worst of a pretty poor bunch.

Pensions mis-selling was effectively called out by the unions. In the face of inadequate regulatory redress schemes, they took some test cases to court. Clear and trenchant judgments soon persuaded the regulator (the PIA/SIB at the time) to set up an appropriately un-biased redress scheme.

SME's however, have no union, and their representative bodies (e.g., the FSB) appear to have done little to address this problem. Accordingly, the banks (and those who have supported the banks' covert recapitalisation), believe that they have "won". But the SME's have shown their views by reacting in a different way – they have withdrawn from the borrowing market. Ruling rates of under 1% indicate that demand is dead. British entrepreneurs do not trust British banks anymore. British businesses have voted with their feet, and the demand for "hedged" loans has dropped through the floor.

I saw a new expression today, in connection with a scam that netted £113 million over 2 ½ years – the police described this as "tradecraft" – where the skill applied to setting up and working the 'con' was compared to that used by terrorist organisations. The "tradecraft" used by banks in swap mis-selling appears to have generally been of a high level – implying that approval for the scam went quite high-up in the bank. There were, however, some notable exceptions:

— the bank that got the client to cover *them* against interest rate rises (how does *that* hedging work? See Chapter 5).
— the salesmen and sales supporters who put in writing "So where are interest rates going to go", against the forward curve, giving cast iron evidence that their behaviour was misleading, either intentionally, or through ignorance.
— the incredible statements in fixed rate loan documents (see Chapter 10).
— sloppiness (in the example at the end of this chapter).

The list goes on.

The other neologism is "de-crimed". Banks think they have now achieved that.

Sadly, dishonesty is now so tightly woven into the fabric of British banks, that it may prove impossible for them to distinguish between right from wrong. Those banks' places will be taken by honest funders and bankers, crowd funders, and other finance providers. A flat economy, high unemployment and both economic and physical depression will ensue, while new national order of lending processes is established. The Brexit vote, depression driven, will seem trivial by comparison.

The flaw is that the banking community will not say "sorry – we got this wrong – how can we help to sort it out?" From the start, there has been one real message – "So we screwed you. So what? We can do this. So, you can stay screwed". In a way, this is understandable. The price of honesty may actually be too much to bear – the shadow of RBS, with its weak finances, its crapulous reputation, and its reliance on covert government patronage in the form of light touch regulation until (as they hope) it is sold off, sets the standard, or lack of it, for the whole industry. Throwing large sums of money into the markets in order to "kick start" the economy has failed abysmally – no-one wants to come out to play. There appears to be no way out. Barring some radically new inspired measures, we are set for continued doldrums for some time to come.

EXAMPLE
THE "MINIMAX" – AN EARLY TALE OF MIS-SELLING – SARUMDALE AND BARCLAYS BANK

The final real life story in this book is one of the most horrible to tell – two men who broke away from their employment in the pub and brewing industry to set up on their own. In the course of making their loans, Barclays sold them no less than *five* interest rate derivatives. The information disclosed in connection with each one is interesting. What is also interesting is the timing of the first sale – well before disclosing that the swap's capital position was secured by the loan covenants – see below. The table illustrating these derivatives is as follows:

PRODUCT	TRADE DATE	SIZE	TERM IN YEARS
Collar	2 January 2001	£4.2 million	4 ¾
Structured Collar	7 February 2006	£5.2 million	10
Structured Collar	3 March 2006	£900,000	10
Structured Collar	9 November 2006	£1.3 million	10
Swap	29 January 2009	£700,000	6
Swap	13 May 2009	£350,000	10 (deferred for 1 year)

The first of these derivatives was described as a "minimax", the cutesy jargon that banks used to describe what they sold. This was sold, according to Sarumdale, via a late approach (when the directors had few possible alternatives), and a heavy "person to person" sell.

The borrower was lucky in that instance – the immediate rate never fell to a degree that payments needed to be made – and the forward curve never caused enough grief for the bank to need to interfere with the business.

The earlier sales slides contain the "usual" error that you should take out a structured collar if you think rates are going to *fall* (!)

Barclays sold Sarumdale less than five additional derivatives over the following eight years – three in 2006, when mis-selling was in its heyday, and two in 2009, when the market had clearly turned.

What is more interesting is the statement in the May 2009 sales slides:

"The hedge can be executed at any point after the loan draw down and security taken, as the credit risk in the contract is covered by the loan's security"

This certainly gives the lie to any statements regarding the independence of the loan and swap contracts!

Finally, I have compiled a graph including the effect of ALL of the swap contracts sold by Barclays to Sarumdale.

The black line is the market value of the derivatives on issue at any point in time, and hits a low of £1/2 million around February 2009. However, adding on collateralisation (grey line) gives the figure to be around £1.5 million then.

Familiar names crop up in the story – the bank Barclays "Business Recovery Specialist", Fiona McDonald, Barclays "Angel of Death" (the RBS equivalent was Aileen Taylor), and Barclays' insolvency practitioner Begbies Traynor, who were all too keen to provide an "independent business review" at a substantial fee, were present.

Fiona McDonald apparently stated that the IRHP's presented her with additional risk, and increased their lending margin by 1%. On other cases of hers I have seen, the IRHP miraculously escapes mention.

The narrative ends as follows, as does mine on this case:

> "Two days following our meeting (delivering a letter of complaint to Barclays), Begbies arrived at our offices to take control of our business".

I can do no better than to quote three tweets:

> 28 October 2015: *"Shit day today. My partner died. Worked with him 25 years building company from zero. Stress? IRHP sale! Thanks, bank! Twats! Proud?"*

29 October 2015: *"Thanks for all kind messages. Appreciated! He was a great man friend and partner."*

9 November 2015: *"Partners funeral today. Caused by stress in my view at loss of our business. IRHP! Protect bank, that's all. Another to brush under carpet."*

AFTERWORD

Interest rate swap mis-selling, and the group ignorance which surrounds the issue, has caused enormous damage to businesses, their financial soundness, their employees, their prospects, and their very existence, in many cases. The government and its agencies miscalculated badly when they thought the issue could be resolved by a quick "flip" of RBS back into the private sector, and a slow bank recapitalisation driven by a secret and sustained programme of what many would see as extortion and destruction. The penalty has been the withdrawal of demand for borrowing, which continues to decimate the UK's economic prospects. Without the entrepreneur class willing to borrow from such banks, economic expansion remains at a flat lining level, holding back recovery and restricting tax funds to government.

The bankers and their dishonesty have won…. but at a terrible cost. Also, my bet is that none of them will ever tell the truth publicly about what they have done.

Banks have recently restarted "plugging" swaps – targeting inter alia, GP practices.

When will it ever end?

APPENDIX A
DARA O'BRIAIN'S CHIP GAME
- 'SCHOOL OF HARD SUMS'

"You and your mate have a bag containing 65 chips. You take turns to each take between one and seven chips, and the person who takes the last chip has to do a dance. Should you go first or second, and what dance would you do?"

First – the answer itself is very simple. You should always go second. The number of chips you take on each turn is mandatory – you take the number that, when added to the number your mate just took, adds to eight. Then, after each even numbered turn, the total number removed is a multiple of eight.

Accordingly, the total removed progresses as follows (clearly only counting every second turn) – 8,16,24,32.... , and so on, up to 64. At that point, your mate is left with only one choice – take the last chip, and lose.

Clearly, the numbers 65 and seven in the problem have been chosen beforehand to give the required answer.

If you played this game with someone, and made no attempt to disguise your moves, they would probably work out after two or three games exactly what was going on. To put this into context, consider the following:

1)   I want to teach the game to my eight year old son, or
2)   I want to use it to persuade someone to gamble and lose

For 1), the easiest way is to use an 8x8 chessboard. Put 64 of the chips one in each square, and the one left over on the side. Suggest that, as the total of each even numbered turn add to eight, all chips are taken from the same row, as far as is possible. It will become clear that the one on the side will fall to be taken by the player going first.

However, if we desire to win money by duplicitous betting, we approach things far differently. The trick would be to play the game for a number of small bets, allowing the other party to win a few. The idea is to lull him into a sense of security by letting him think that it is a game of skill. By taking a suboptimal number of chips, the second player can pass the winning initiative over to his partner. He can also "steer" himself into a losing position. At the end, he suggests "one big bet" to finish things off. "I'll even let you go first" he says.

Now, imagine the slides that a bank might create in order to sell this game in the same way it sold swaps. There would be lots of ideas of "strategies" and "tactics" in order to get down from 53 chips to 29, etc, etc, and lots of other such nonsense. This would be designed to hide the fact that the game is fixed from the outset.

The swaps game is very similar. A bank lends money, imposes loan covenants, then force-sells a swap which can break those covenants. It does not predefine what its actions would be if the swap itself broke those covenants. This is a dishonest way of carrying on business.

APPENDIX B
TYPICAL PRESENTATION
SLIDES

SLIDES, FOLLOWED BY MY COMMENTS

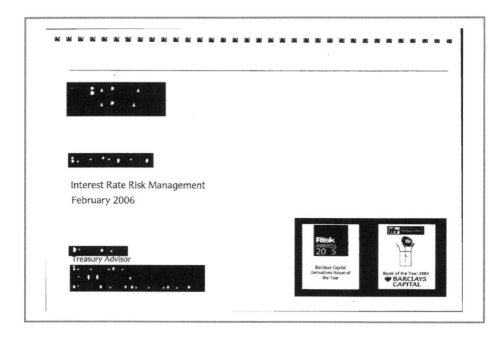

Large print is designed to give the impression that you are being advised – later small print reverses this.

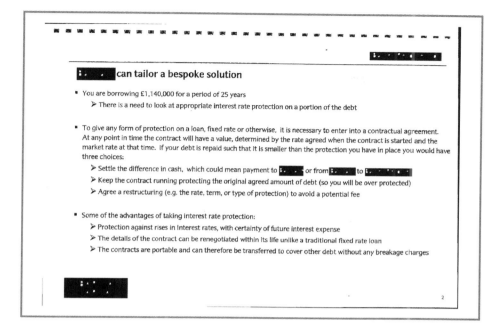

Note the ambiguous language:

"There is a need to look at appropriate interest rate protection…

Whose need is it? Not the bank's – banks see floating rates as safe.

Not yours – you are taking on extra risk – floating rates are there for a reason!

The next block is OK, apart from the ambiguous word "protection"

The third block is seriously misleading.

"Protection against rises in interest rates" does not mention the fact that rates are considered as a string of rates into the future, rather than just single number. If the longer-term rates fall while short-term rates rise, cash flow is protected, but the capital losses mount. THEY CANNOT BE IGNORED!

Renegotiation – your ability to renegotiate depends on your capital position, which, if negative, clearly ties your hands. Any fixed rate term loans can be renegotiated at any time, if the bank agrees. This sentence is nonsense!

The portability point is contrary to other parts of the sales spiel – if "protection" for a loan (as the bank calls it) is so important, why should you lose it by moving it to another loan? Nonsense, again.

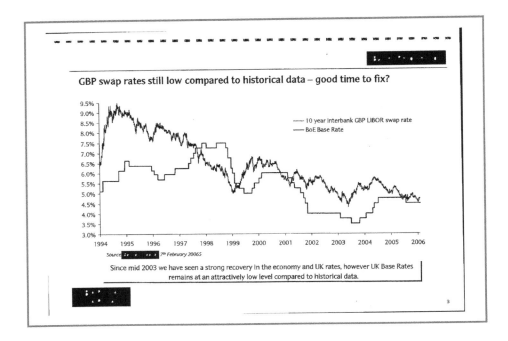

The graph shows a twelve-year history of rates back to 1994.

Wording – "GBP Swap rates still low compared to historic data–good time to fix?"

This slide is part of the Gordon Brown subtext, to assume that rates will go from falling to rising again. In fact, the bank is looking at far more valuable information itself - the forward trading curve. This indicates pessimism in the market, in the shape of longer-term lower rates. Note – this graph does not show the timing of future falls.

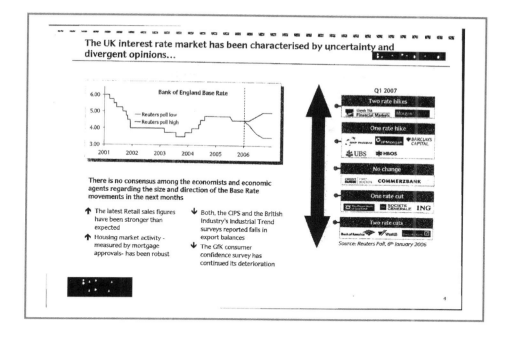

It should be noted that short-term forecasts are shown – economists rarely try and forecast in excess of 1-2 years in this way. Here, the bank is holding out that these short-term forecasts are a good basis for a 25-year lock-in! This is highly misleading.

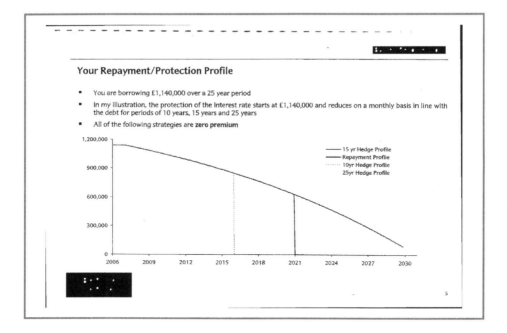

Your Repayment/Protection Profile

- You are borrowing £1,140,000 over a 25 year period
- In my illustration, the protection of the interest rate starts at £1,140,000 and reduces on a monthly basis in line with the debt for periods of 10 years, 15 years and 25 years
- All of the following strategies are **zero premium**

This graph simply shows the outstanding capital under the loan, which is mirrored by the level at which the swap has been designed.

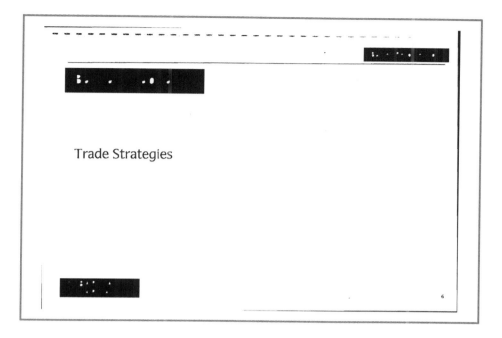

Heading Page

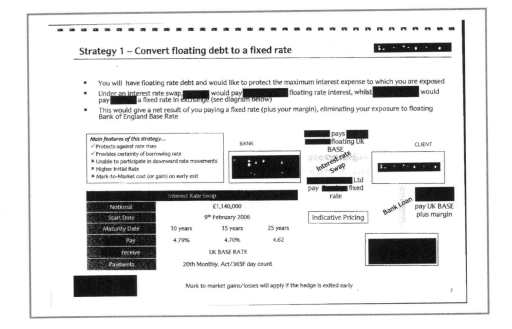

Cash flows under a "swap plus loan" are described. However, banks see fixed rates as risk, not hedging. Therefore, this and the following two slides are very misleading.

The small print comment at the bottom of the slide – "Mark to market gains/losses will apply if the hedge is exited early", does not fully describe the continuous capital drag that the swap puts on the business. The swap can break the loan covenants – and put your company into GRG at any time– even if the current base rate does not fall!

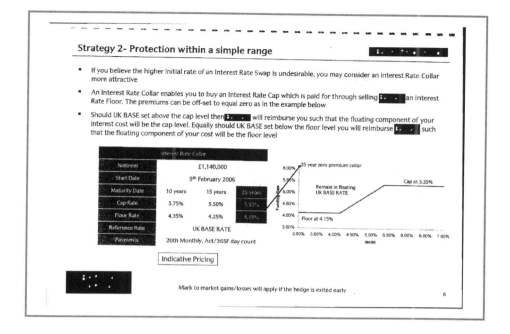

Again, cash flow issues are described reasonably well, but the slide is designed to conceal the capital risk.

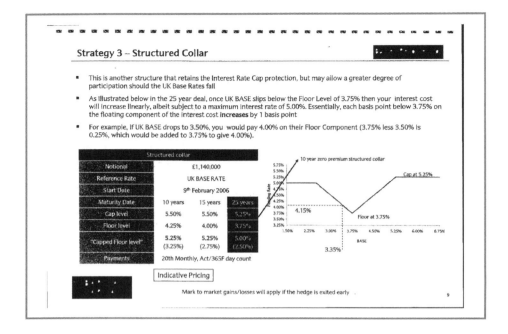

This product is designed to provide non-negative cash flow for the borrower in the early months (hopefully, years), but expose him to the risk of future negative ones, as determined by the forward trading curve.

Swaps are less attractive to buyers in more optimistic times, as it is difficult to achieve bank profitability and non-negative client flows at the same time. The structured collar pushes risk into the later term of the contract, and reduces earlier negative cash flows.

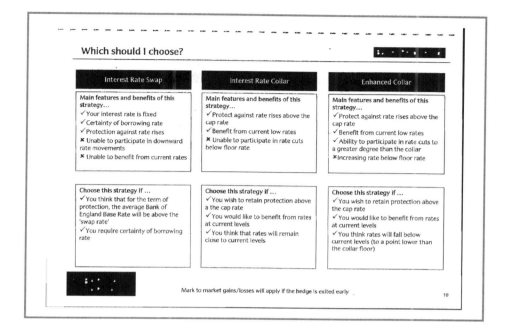

Pros and cons for each product are summarised.

Again, capital issues are ignored. The text recommends a swap based on the future expectations average of average rates. There is more to it than this – an unfavourable rate shape in the early years may render the business insolvent, even if rates subsequently improve.

There is an error in the last box, where it says, (for the Structured Collar) – "Choose this strategy if... You think rates will fall below current levels to a point lower than the collar floor. "

This is the polar opposite of the truth.

For any of these contracts, falls in the immediate interest rate will cause cash flow damage, and falls in the forward curve will cause capital damage.

179

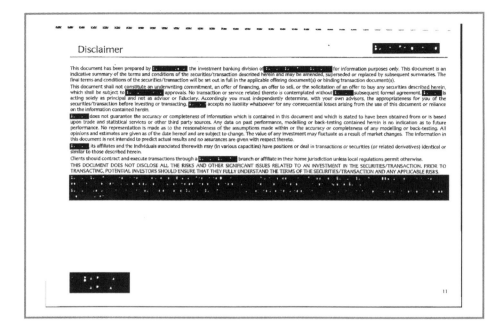

A set of general disclaimers, but, most specifically, in capital letters at the end, the fact that all risks are not disclosed, and that the buyer should ensure that they understand all the risks.

By reducing disclosure of the universal capital risks inherent in these products to the absolute minimum, and not using a Credit Support Annex, the process is clearly designed to mislead the borrower as to the downsides of all of these products.

Printed in Germany
by Amazon Distribution
GmbH, Leipzig

16314413R00110